THE ART & CRAFT OF THE
SHORT STORY

THE ART & CRAFT OF THE
SHORT
STORY

RICK DeMARINIS

STORY PRESS

Cincinnati, OH
www.writersdigest.com

04 03 02 01 00   5 4 3 2 1

Library of Congress Cataloging-in-Publication Data

DeMarinis, Rick
  The art & craft of the short story / by Rick DeMarinis.—1st ed.
    p. cm.
  Includes index.
  ISBN 1-88491-045-9 (hardcover : alk. paper)
    1. Short story—Authorship. I. Title: The art and craft of the short story.
  II. Title.
  PN3373.D37 2000
  808.3'1—dc21   00-023150
                                                                      CIP

Design by Clare Finney
Cover photography by Masao Mukai/Photonica

A shorter version of "A Writer's Education" was published in *The Writer* magazine.

James Wright's "A Blessing" from *The Branch Will Not Break* © 1963 by James Wright, Wesleyan University Press. Used by permission of University Press of New England.

My thanks to my wife, Carole Bubash, who read this with a sharp and unsparing eye, and to John Quinn for the use of his fabulous floating library.

CONTENTS

A WRITER'S EDUCATION

I wasn't raised in a family of book readers. My mother worked in a fish cannery and my stepfather drove a bread truck. There were a few books in the house—a library copy of *Forever Amber* no one had bothered to return; some mildewed paperbacks with racy covers; a beat-up leather-bound encyclopedia that expressed awe over a recent engineering miracle, the Eiffel Tower; and, amazingly, a beautiful, gold-embossed, wonderfully illustrated copy of *The Life of Mohammed*. (My mother was a fallen-away Lutheran, my stepfather a nonchurchgoing Baptist, and I, at fifteen, was a part-time Catholic and a full-time skeptic.) This small and exotic collection of books didn't make much sense, but it contained an essential message for a young aspiring writer: Don't expect things to make sense. Expect surprise.

In my high school English class, we were introduced to something called, with unmistakable reverence, Literature. I hated it. I remember having to read novels such as *Silas Marner* and *Giants in the Earth*. But the nebulous minds of fifteen-year-old California kids were hardly prepared for such fare. We traded ragged copies of Mickey Spillane's Mike Hammer novels out in the parking lot, away from the snooping eyes of teachers. A novel about gang warfare called *The Amboy Dukes* was hugely popular with us. We saw such fiction as extensions of our internal lives and could not make the great leap into the worlds of Eliot and Rölvaag. I'm a lot older and

1

a little wiser now, but I still expect what I read to be an extension of my internal life. If it doesn't resonate with something in me, I read with the same reluctance I had when I was fifteen.

Something happens to people destined for a life of writing that has nothing to do with Literature. It happens early in life and is probably the psychological equivalent of scarlet fever. It has to do with pain. In answer to the question, "What is the best early training for a writer?" Hemingway said, "An unhappy childhood." Unhappy children (unhappy for whatever reasons—from physical abuse to psychological abandonment) grow up with the potentially destructive feeling that they have to *seize* the right to exist. They have been told in subtle and unsubtle ways that they have no rightful claim on life. These are the ones who get in trouble early and then go on to achieve impressive things, either good or bad—the criminals and artists, the psychopaths and the self-made millionaires. An unhappy childhood often hones a powerful sense of injustice, and that very often is the core motivation for reformers, overachievers, criminals and artists. Dickens did not choose his subjects randomly; he was well acquainted with desperation and the torments of poverty.

People who grow up feeling justified and at home in their worlds can settle for less, having never felt the urge to pull things apart or to put them together again in gratifying ways. On the other hand, I know that people who have had wonderful childhoods have become first-rate writers in spite of this handicap (Eudora Welty comes to mind). Writers who had loving and protective parents, who never knew grinding poverty or emotional deprivation cannot be dismissed as "not having suffered enough" to qualify for the trade. *Something* happened to them. Maybe birth was trauma enough. Someone responsive to his or her surroundings, responsive in the sense of always being intensely aware, of noticing the details, of having no protective layers of dullness and disinterest, someone who is continuously being affected by the force of these impressions—that is, a person destined to be an artist or a psychiatric patient—will find a wrenching experience waiting around every corner. A childhood doesn't have to be lousy to be traumatizing. As Flannery O'Connor said, in regard to what one needs to know in order to become a writer, ". . . anybody who has survived his childhood has enough information about life to last him the rest of his days."

Then something else happens. We find that words can be an escape from the pain of social impotence. Words became, for me, a bright mantle of power. I discovered that pressing a no. 2 pencil into a sheet of clean white paper was a sensual experience. And as that pencil moved, a world was created. How amazing! (It's probably no coincidence that this impulse typically occurs right about the time of puberty.)

Creating fictional worlds is a natural refuge for the powerless, since it *confers* power. There on the clean white page, all power is restored. My English teachers—except for that special teacher all of us seem to encounter, that "mythic helper" who appears just at the right time with the right kind of encouragement—had no perceivable passion for words, no respect for their rough or delicate strengths. With them, it was as if the literature they asked us to read was made of rarefied ideas breathed directly onto the page by pure mind from the high crags of Mount Olympus. They never once suggested that a human being with a quill or typewriter put the words down one by one with agony and joy.

The clatter and bang, the wheeze and chuff—the untamed music of our flexible language—moved me like small earthquakes. Rarefied ideas were a vapor that would be condensed in college and graduate school much later. Besides, as a young teenager, I had no apparatus for absorbing serious ideas and surely none for expressing them. Writing was a physical exercise, as pleasureful as bench-pressing heavy weights, but not as socially acceptable.

My English teachers and I regarded each other through the wrong ends of our private telescopes. We shied away from each other, each perceiving the other as a possible enemy. And yet they gave me an occasional B or A for my awkward but imaginatively untethered "essays" and "stories" that twisted the world out of its expected shapes.

This habit of twisting the world persisted. If you twist hard and long, guided by intuition, it surrenders its truths. George Eliot knew

3

that, Chekhov knew that, Joyce knew that. Everyone who has persisted in this art eventually comes to know that.

At first, short stories seemed the easiest of the narrative arts, the easiest way to become a writer. Why on earth did I think that? Well, because short stories were *short*. The novel seemed out of reach. How could anyone write a novel? Might as well decide to add a head to Mount Rushmore. You had to write four, five hundred *pages* to make a novel. Clearly, the short story was an easier form, the poem even easier.

My attitude has changed radically. I'm convinced now that the shorter the form, the more difficult it is to write something worthwhile in it. (Emphasis here on *worthwhile*.) The novel will consume more of your time and calories, but I believe it's harder to write a good short story than it is to write a good novel. Maybe this is prejudice. I don't think so. I've written eight novels (six published) and hundreds of short stories, and writing the novels—once the characters were in place and the story line more or less figured out— was like riding a runaway train. Short stories, however, always test my intuitive ability, my vision, my access to inspiration. These are the same uncompromising tests poets are subject to. (The poem, the most unforgiving of literary forms, lays the intelligence and vision of the poet naked. It will not suffer sloppy writing.)

I've read a lot of comparative definitions of the novel and short story, many of which boil down to the truism: The novel is a long narrative, the short story not so long. Some have even used word-count limits as the ultimate dividing line: Anything over forty thousand words is a novel. Anything less than twenty thousand words is a short story. The no-man's-land in between belongs by default to the novella. I don't think this quantitative approach helps much. Frank O'Connor, in his study of the short story, *The Lonely Voice*, made a useful distinction. "For some reason that I can only guess at," he says, "the novel is bound to be a process of identification between the reader and the character. . . . One character at least in any novel must represent the reader in some aspect of his own conception of himself—as the Wild Boy, the Rebel, the Dreamer, the Misunderstood Idealist. . . ." The short story, however, "has never had a hero."

I like to think of "Cinderella" as an archetypal novel form. Cinderella, victim of her stepmother's and stepsisters' cruelty, eventually triumphs because of her superior beauty and steadfast moral qualities. At every stage of Cinderella's ordeal, the reader identifies with her struggle. And her eventual triumph is the reader's triumph.

The short story, however, might drop in on Cinderella twenty years after her marriage to the Prince. We see them at home, watching TV, eating TV dinners, wondering where Princess Debby is and why she finds it necessary to run around with that offensive commoner Joe Bob McQuirk on his motorcycle. Cinderella and Prince don't talk to each other very much these days. The monarchy has been overthrown, and Prince has long overspent his inheritance. The unpaid bills and letters from the collection agency are stacked on the kitchen table. Prince hammers down champagne cocktails for breakfast. He's forty pounds overweight, often forgets to bathe, and Cinderella's beauty is fading. She's lonely and thinking of leaving Prince, but where can she go . . . ? This is the essence of the modern short story. It takes a hard close-up look at small bits of life. It does not lend itself to sentimentality and romance.

". . . it might be truer to say," O'Connor continues, "that while we often read a familiar novel for companionship, we approach the short story in a very different mood. It is more akin to the mood of Pascal's saying: *Le silence eternel de ces espaces infinis m'effraie*."

The short story at its best examines a pivotal moment in a life, whether it is one of spiritual crisis or domestic ennui, with an unflinching gaze. Consequently, says O'Connor, "The storyteller . . . must be much more of a writer, much more of an artist . . ." than the novelist. More, in any case, of a poet.

A CAVEAT AND A
CONFESSION

You write the short story for love—not for money, fame, or tenure. Love is the only acceptable motive. (Love can sometimes be obsession. In writing, the two are synonymous.) There was a time when you could compromise your love with economic need: Fifty years ago, a professional writer could make a decent living writing nothing but short stories. There was a healthy plethora of magazines in the United States, each paying good money. Fifty years ago, it was possible to be paid several thousand dollars by a major magazine for a single short story. *Redbook*, in 1949, published six short stories per issue, a continuing serial, as well as a *complete novel*.

I recently picked up a 1947 *Good Housekeeping* in a New Mexico thrift store. It has a prize-winning story in it by a writer named Allan Seager. He was paid five thousand dollars for it. (I know this because the amount was announced on the first page of the story.) Five thousand dollars in 1947 is the equivalent of twenty to thirty thousand now. Magazines such as *Collier's*, *The Saturday Evening Post*, *Good Housekeeping*, *The American Mercury*, *McCall's*, *Esquire*, *Bluebook*, and *Redbook* published from two to eight stories an issue. If you sold three or four stories a year back in that heyday, you might have enough money to pay your rent, keep your larder stocked, make payments on the Studebaker, and have something left over for a Florida vacation. Why? Because magazine fiction, along with the movies and radio, was a major source of entertainment for the general public. Short story writers cranked them out to feed America's insatiable appetite for diversion. Reader interest was tweaked by blurbs under a story's title.

> *There may be a girl who is ready to do almost anything—just to prove to a guy that two can live closer than one*

> *A young girl's first dance . . . her first heartbreak . . . and her father's dilemma*

> *A ring on her finger . . . the years slipping by. How safe can a man make the future? . . . How long can a girl wait?*

These were simple, formulaic stories meant only to entertain, and the subscribers loved them.

There were critics who deplored this sort of market-oriented approach to the short story. Kenneth Allan Robinson, back in 1924, complained, "The American short story has been developed into a vast national industry, standardized like all vast industries, and turning out a standardized product. The mechanical elements of story construction have been so over-stressed that story-writing has come to be regarded as a purely mechanical process, something that is perfectly demonstrable. The result has been a product of high and soulless excellence."

THE SHORT STORY'S RAISON D'ETRE

Market conditions have changed. Magazine fiction has yielded its vast audience to television. The reading public has gradually become a watching public. This is both a disaster and a gift. Freed of needing to satisfy a specific audience with specific expectations, the short story has blossomed beyond the constraints a strong commercial market imposes. Most quality short stories today are published in the literary quarterlies. The high-paying, slick-paper magazines that still print short stories are few in number—you can count them on your fingers—and only rarely do they print more than one story per issue.

But this is demography, an evolution of the modes of entertainment fostered and determined by technology. You, as a writer of short stories, can dismiss it. In the wake of national trends, your love may have become quaint, but the short story is not obsolete. It remains an important art form. Its brief and surgical insights are indispensable to a culture that needs them, perhaps more than ever. The short story—unruly, sharp-eyed, exacting—will not roll over and die under an insipid electronic glow. Anton Chekhov, a progenitor of the modern short story, said, "Man will become better only when you make him see what he is like." This is a lofty goal, but I believe it is art's unique and original purpose.

RULE ONE: THERE ARE NO RULES

You must love the short story, but you must also fear it. The ideal story, like a dream lover, is unattainable. I guess that's the nature of the attraction. And, like a dream lover, it cannot be a tidy and cooperative entity, something that can be made compliant by specific lists of dos and don'ts. Good writers will break every rule that attempts to concretize some aspect of it. Every story makes its own rules. Each time I sit down to compose one, I feel at sea. All my previous experience and knowledge abandons me. I am a novice again, hoping, even praying, for the insights and inspirations that make composition possible.

But shouldn't a story meet certain obvious and universal requirements? Shouldn't it be *intelligible* on some immediate level, the narrative ordering of events sequential, as they appear to be ordered in real life? Shouldn't it have characters who move the action forward to a resonant conclusion? Shouldn't dialogue contribute to our understanding of the characters and not just consist of idle vocalizations? Shouldn't a story be "shown" in scenes and descriptive passages, rather than in a narration that only "tells"? And shouldn't there be concrete renderings of the environs in which the story takes place so that the reader can visualize and thus inhabit the story?

I can't object to these basic requirements. They seem reasonable enough. But talented writers will always have occasion to violate one or more of them. "The Yellow Raft" by Evan S. Connell is a story *without characters* that nonetheless has an emotional punch. Robert Coover's "The Babysitter" takes sequential narrative and stands it on its head. "A Questionnaire for Rudolph Gordon" by Jack Matthews is an affective piece that has no dialogue, characters, *or* narrative: The inferences we draw from an apparently impersonal questionnaire suggest the life of a man we never see but who nevertheless attracts our empathy. Raymond Carver wrote a splendid little story called "Mr. Coffee and Mr. Fixit." This story is told in narrative, its only dialogue coming in its last two lines, an exchange so desperately forlorn you immediately understand that dialogue in any other part of the story would be too much to bear. It's a story than can only be told in a series of minimalist declaratives that act as a kind of containment shield. If the story had been openly dramatized, presented in scenes—with dialogue, full of descriptive detail, thick with atmosphere—it would go over the top, it would get explosively crazy fast, perhaps impossible to manage.

I promised you a confession. This is it: I don't know how to write a short story even though I've written hundreds of them, published five collections of them, sold them to magazines, both literary and commercial. I have also taught the subject for more than twenty years in various university English departments that hired me for that purpose. But here's the thing: I don't have a set of rules, a formula, a system, that tells me how to set about writing a story of *literary quality*. I don't have a "how." If I had such a system, one that would fit every interesting human situation, I'd write a prizewinner every day of the week. I'd make Chekhov look like a backslider. I'd make Cheever look like he was working out laundry lists. I'd make Hemingway look punch-drunk. But the hard truth is that there is no system, no set of rules that guarantee able composition or abundant production. There is no magic formula that will make hard work, commitment, inspiration, taste, and good luck unnecessary. To paraphrase a quip of Somerset Maugham's: There are three rules for writing a short story. Unfortunately, no one knows what they are. Maugham was talking about the novel, but his words apply to all the arts. On the same subject, Flannery O'Connor said this: "As soon as a writer 'learns to write,' as soon as he knows what he is going to find, and discovers a way to say what he knew all along, or worse still, a way to say nothing, he is finished."

THE ONE AND ONLY TRICK

Back in 1905, the literary critic William Patten wrote this about the nature of the short story.

> From the time of Poe and Hawthorne the nature and limitations of the short story have formed a favorite subject of discussion among writers and critics of fiction. And the controversy has been all the more valuable because no definite conclusions have ever been arrived at. Had there been a general agreement as to a definition, the short story might now be as dead as the sonnet.

I think it can be safely said that in 2105 no definite conclusions will have been reached about the nature and limitations of the short story. Every living art form exists in an evolutionary stage; when its evolution stops, it quickly becomes a fossil, interesting only to curators and scholars.

That said, I do know this: I can tell you how a story can go wrong. I can tell you certain things every writer of successful short stories knows. I can suggest some things that may squeeze the trigger of your loaded imagination. It's even possible that some of the things I've learned in the past thirty-odd years may help you. In the following pages, I will do my best to accomplish exactly that. I will tell you what I know. Maybe I can give you some pointers that will save you some wasted effort and time. That's what I've done as a writing teacher in several universities. I keep getting hired and have never been sent packing, so I guess I've done something right. Some of my students have published both short stories and novels. I don't take credit for their success. They were obsessed with the need to write. They worked hard. They were patient with themselves. They had all the qualifications they needed before they stepped into my classroom. I like to think I did *some*thing for them. I like to think I at least gave them useful advice at a moment when they could best use it. I hope I can, throughout this book, do the same for you.

But I'm not a cheerleader. I won't give you a pep talk. The writing life is hard. Too many people who took the vows when I did have wound up in their fifties and sixties collecting aluminum or pumping gas for a living. There were times when I collected aluminum, applied for and received food stamps, depended on the generosity of friends. My dedication to this work became a ticket to poverty. I hated the way some people looked at me when I peeled food stamps out of my wallet in the Safeway checkout line. I'd buy Danish hams and pricey coffee just to annoy them. I was mad at a world that did not reward me for my creative efforts. My daughter wondered why her clothes had to be handmade or taken from the racks of Goodwill Industries. My wife took menial jobs so that we could make the rent. She often came home angry and depressed from having to deal with people who treated her like furniture. We lived in a context of resentment. Sometimes the resentment turned inward, threatening to sour our marriage. It didn't. I'm thankful for that.

I don't care for books that light candles for the blind. You know what I mean: "Tap into your God-given creativity after six easy lessons." Can you imagine a book that suggests you can be a high-wire artist? "Yes, you can do it! You can conquer your fear of heights and your genetic tendency toward vertigo! There is money to be made dancing on a wire forty feet above a circus floor!" As a writing teacher, I begin each class with a caveat: Do this only if you can't imagine your life not doing it. Do this because you are obsessed. *Do this for love.*

I expect, however, that you are already committed to this difficult and often thankless work and don't need cheerleading or caveats. Fine. You are my brother or sister in our mutual dedication to a demanding art form. I expect that you already know you possess this elusive quality called talent. (Remember the ninth grade? Weren't *you* the one who could string outrageous sentences together that made your teacher squint suspiciously at you?) And maybe you've heard that talent isn't everything. It isn't. It's important— you've got to have some mastery of the language, some ability to put words into sequences that charm, chill, and illuminate. But even abundant talent can't survive a lack of stubborn perseverance. Theodore Dreiser had a relatively modest talent, but that did not stop him from becoming a major American realist.

Gustave Flaubert's advice is worth remembering: "Talent is long patience." Writers of modest talent have become great successes because of their patient refusal to buckle under daunting pressures. To continue in spite of rejection and the many hectoring demands on your time and energy, this is the one and only trick.

2

THE SEA OF STORIES: WHERE STORIES COME FROM

Stories come from dreams, waking and sleeping. They come from life, yours and the lives of others.

Human beings can't live without stories, just as they can't live without dreaming. Storytelling is how we make sense of the world. Each of us knows instinctively that we live in a context of mystery, that no explanation of existence—what governs our behavior and determines our fates—will completely pacify our restless and solitary selves. We know that the world is made of dazzling opaque surfaces, that we are margined on all sides by oblivion, and that our situation, however secure, is frighteningly vulnerable. Any vagrant wind can blow down your house of cards.

This intuitive grasp of how things are allows the writer to see, compassionately, into the human predicament, the predicament of men and women who find themselves, at particular crossroads in their lives, afflicted by doubts, demoralized by crises, or deluded by false values. And the writer is responsible for the fate of these characters. It's a responsibility not to be accepted lightly. The writer has to make what happens to them make sense. In the chaos of random events, the writer looks for a meaning.

Out of a kindred impulse, the man in the street will tell you his life story if you give him the chance. He needs little encouragement. It's the human thing to do. The urge is a reflex triggered by the sympathetic glance, the accepting smile, the unguarded pause; we can't help ourselves. Give the stranger an opening, and here comes the deluge.

We live in a sea of stories. We are so accustomed to this sea we don't even notice it except when it irritates us. The man seated next to you on a plane will tell you about his job, his vacation plans, his wife, his kids, the degeneration of national mores, and even his illnesses. He may become alarmingly earnest and confide to you his fears and desires. Sometimes the deeply personal information is given cautiously, disguised by what the teller thinks is humor.

Most of the time such stories are only boring and inconsequential. But even then they have a purpose. The purpose is not to entertain you, the trapped listener, but to let the storyteller make his own life specific and orderly so that he can see how it plays to a disinterested audience. And because this story is always biased, because he slants the story so that it favors himself, it is inevitably a fiction. The man on the plane is lying (though he may not know it), but hidden in his fiction is need, and need is always truthful. He needs your sympathy and approval. He wants to be understood. If he has an ax to grind, he'll want to see if you are an ally or an enemy. These stories, fascinating or dull, weld you together into a community of two. Great stories written by the masters weld us into a community of millions. Melville, Tolstoy, Chekhov, Kafka, Joyce, Woolf, Hemingway—the list is much longer—have shaped the way we perceive ourselves in this existence.

BOTTOM'S DREAM

I have an aunt who tells stories nonstop without prologue or segues, but they are always interesting. She knows a man, married fifty-four years, who saved a million dollars. He had, in old age, become an invalid. His wife nursed him, washed him, fed him, worked like a slave for him. But when he died, he left his money to his brother, and some even went to a sister in Europe, a sister he'd never seen. His wife got nothing. She had to borrow five thousand dollars to have him buried. My aunt told this story because the pure injustice of it made it interesting. We sat in my mother's kitchen, shaking our heads over our coffees in disbelief. "Some *people*," she finally said, a judgment and coda. "Go figure," I said, beginning to figure a story based on the old man and his widow. But my aunt had already launched into another story.

These everyday dramas need to be held up to the light again and again, but they remain opaque without an artful structure that catalyzes them into transparency. As told, the light of meaning never shines through them. Providing the catalyzing structure is the fiction writer's job. My aunt is possessed by the unrelieved injustice of the widow's story, but after she tells it, she can only shake her head, her anger transformed by time into sad bewilderment. "Some *people*," she says.

Such stories cannot go untold. I'm sure my aunt has repeated it dozens of times by now. It's one of life's dark little nuggets. I've repeated it myself several times to friends, embellished with fictive details.

Here's another one, told to me by my friend Ingrid, who works in a boutique. An elderly man comes in often, heads straight for Ingrid. He won't talk to other salespersons. He always asks about expensive soaps—which one is the best buy. Even though these imported soaps come in boxes of two, he asks if he might have them separately gift wrapped. He comes in three, four times a week on a soap-buying mission. Obviously he's interested not so much in soap as he is in Ingrid. He's been trying to impress her that either he knows his soaps or that he is a clean old man. I suggest to Ingrid, over dinner, that the old rounder wants her to give him a bath. Ingrid's eyes widen at the thought, then she remembers another story, another place and time, another man. She had been recently divorced, and was living alone in a small town in New England, a fishing town. One night a man came to her door, a man she didn't know but had seen around town. He was a fisherman. On the night of his unannounced visit he was wearing overalls and rubber boots. He reeked of haddock and bourbon. He looked like Ahab, just off the reeling deck.

"This is your lucky day," he said. He had a fancy jar under his arm. "I'm going to give you a lovely bubble bath," he said.

"This is *your* lucky day," Ingrid said. "There's no bathtub in this apartment." Ingrid shoved the drunk fisherman out of her doorway.

End of story. No coda for it, just stark wonderment at what human beings do with their free time.

Just the other day a carpenter friend of mine told me a story about how he had found $6000 hidden in the wall of a house he was remodeling. The money, in old silver-standard bills, was sealed in a mildewed envelope. The house, it seemed, was once owned by an eccentric gambler. When the new owner was told about the hidden treasure, he tore down all the other walls in the house, looking for more. He didn't find any, and the destruction he caused cost him more than what was found in the old gambler's hidey-hole.

These stories need to be told. We shake our heads at them, our only response to injustice and crazed behavior. We've got to tell them; we've got to hear them. We've got to be reminded again and again how fundamentally bizarre our lives are, how the irrational moves through them like red wind.

And there is no end to them. As Bottom says, in *A Midsummer Night's Dream*, ". . . it shall be called Bottom's Dream, because it hath no bottom." The source of story is deeper than the western Pacific's Marianas Trench.

The fiction writer can take possession of these somewhat extreme situations and construe them to his or her own purposes. The fiction writer will cut into the surface of stories like these and come up with an understanding of their meaning that will illuminate—in some way, and with varying degrees of success—our human predicament. That's what we do. That's the only assignment.

THE WRITER'S NOTEBOOK

So, here is the first *habit*, as a writer of short fiction, you must acquire: Keep a notebook handy so you can record what you hear and see, and so you can record what you think about what you've seen and heard. Too many times I've found myself without paper and pen in a restaurant or bar or plane when something happens that needs to be recorded in detail. I have a sieve for a memory, and too much is lost if I depend on it. I've learned to always carry tools with me.

You may have an inventive imagination, but you can't build a world from scratch. And why should you? Your daily life is loaded with booty. Help yourself. A jungle of invention thrives out there. Respect its offerings by paying very close attention. Henry James said, "Be one of those people on whom nothing is lost." He's talking to *you*.

When I had brain surgery to remove a pituitary tumor a few years ago, I saw every appointment I had with the doctors as an opportunity to gather story material. I was scared as anyone would be facing surgery that could leave me blind, paralyzed, or dead, but I often was able to separate my scared self from my writing self. The doctors didn't know it but my questions were not spurred by the anxiety of someone facing his mortality. I was *interviewing* them. My wife joined me during these sessions. She took copious notes. We studied arcane medical texts together. On The Learning Channel we watched brain surgeons use power saws to open doors into skulls. ("Whoa, look at the skulldust fly!") The end result was that I got a couple of short stories out of the experience—one taken by a major slick-paper magazine for good money, the other by a literary quarterly.

From brain tumors to backyard arguments, nothing should escape your interest. Fill your notebook with images and ideas and scraps of conversation. With incidents and interpretations of incidents. The little notebook in your pocket or purse will be a constant reminder to you to stay alive to your particular world, whether you're in an office, a prison cell, or a suburb. Stay very awake. Learn to see what most pass over.

A few years ago my wife and I were in a rural Arizona town. We took a walk down the streets of a quiet neighborhood. We came upon a girl lying in the middle of the road, daring traffic, although the only traffic we'd seen that morning was an occasional roadrunner, boat-tail grackle, or lizard. She was about sixteen. "What are you doing, honey?" my wife asked. The girl, staring straight up into the uninterrupted blue sky, said, "I'm waiting for something to happen to me."

This pure expression of self-destructive boredom stunned me. After we got her on her feet and slouching off, we hoped toward home, I took out my notebook and recorded the incident. Some time later I understood that her words came from some forbidden area of the psyche that reduces everyday experience to the black-and-white dynamics of mythology: *The girl was tempting fate.*

The moment found its way into one of my short stories. I loved and envied the girl's honest, if suicidal, courage. Her refusal to accept her circumstances, whatever they were, reminded me of Melville's "Bartleby the Scrivener." Like Bartleby, she was recusing herself from any form of social obligation. She seemed to be saying, "I am what I am; do with me what you will." Characters as interesting as these are all around you.

There are no insignificant lives.

THE ESSENTIAL HABIT—A PEP TALK

Okay, I lied. I *am* going to give you a pep talk.

This little tautology can't be repeated too many times: In order to write you must *write*. That's the Big Secret. You've got to sit down at a given time every day and make sentences. Even if you don't feel like it. *Especially* if you don't feel like it. This is the most important habit you need to acquire. It should become an automatic feature of your daily routine. I violate it more often than I care to admit. I always feel guilty when I do. Guilt is good. Guilt is a righteous motivator. Learn to feel guilty when you skip your time to write.

Some of the best things I've written happened when I didn't want to write. I was mentally fatigued, sick, out of sorts, or just bored with myself. Valid excuses come easy. Some people just want to *be* writers—to be *known* as writers. They don't care much for the humbling grunt work. God knows why this is so. I guess they think there's money, fame, and access to a glamorous social life in it.

Good luck to them. They'll need a lot of it. But what they should want, plain and simple, is to *write*.

No matter how busy you are, no matter how harassed by work, family, or economic straits, you need to find a couple of hours every day to put words down on paper. Don't make the mistake of thinking that you need more favorable circumstances, that you'll start writing when your life changes for the better or when you retire. An apprenticeship can last ten years or more. How much time do you have? The clock is ticking.

Your mind is blank? Never mind. My mind is blank most of the time. I've come to understand that a blank mind is sometimes an asset. Important thoughts just get in the way. I don't need them. I need words. I need characters, not ideas. I need situations with good dramatic potential, not philosophy. These things come from the replenishable aquifers of the psyche, below and beyond big ideas and philosophy.

So make it your habit to sit down every day for two hours— three if you can manage it—and write. Seal yourself off from the world. Don't answer the doorbell, don't answer the phone. Never take a cellphone into your place of work. Stay out of range of turned-on televisions and radios. If you can't escape the distractions of ambient noise, get yourself earplugs or use one of those "white noise" machines that cover the random screech and rumble of your environment with benign sounds—Malibu surf, rain in the Ever- glades, Rocky Mountain blizzard. Protect these private hours. If you have a room to work in, hang a big "Let Me Suffer Alone!" sign on the door. And you don't need a room with a view; what you need is the complete freedom of unviolated isolation.

Okay. Now you're alone, sealed off from the world, face-to-face with a stack of virgin white paper—your nemesis and hope. You load your printer, you boot up your word processing program. Your fingers are stiff on the keyboard. The cursor seems to mock you with its steadily winking pulse. Or your old Underwood, that chunk of black iron, sits on your desk like the stone of Sisyphus. This is the moment of truth.

It's an awesome moment because that blank paper represents

the possible—an infinity of choice. How do you choose those first words? Any words will do, but whatever words you choose, you believe (falsely) that they must be *exceptional*. What a burden you've given yourself! After a few minutes of this, you might decide you have nothing worthwhile to say after all. Distracting thoughts flit through your brain like clouds of gnats. (Did I get enough chutney for the chicken curry tonight? Should I winterize the car tomorrow? Why doesn't Mary Lou Stoppovitch like me anymore?)

The great paralyzer, boredom, begins to anesthetize your brain. You're tempted to boot up the solitaire game on your hard drive.

What's the problem here? The problem is that you're thinking of writing as a purely intellectual process: exceptional ideas captured in deathless prose. But in reality, the composition of fiction is more of a physical process. You've got to put your hands on the keyboard, you've got to punch the keys with your determined fingers until words begin to collect.

The very act of writing sentences produces more sentences. And sometimes (not always) these sentences lead you to an inspiration. At which point you say a little prayer of thanks and sail on.

Don't concern yourself with how empty-headed you are or how bored you are. Start putting words up on that screen or down on that paper. If nothing else, attack your empty-headed boredom directly: Write about *it*. Get playful. Writing isn't hard work, it's hard play.

Pushing Through: An Example

I'm bored. I'm bored by everything. Anyone can see that. It's gotten into my posture, my facial expressions, my breathing. I'm so bored I sometimes forget to breathe. Then a surging yawn sweeps over me as my body becomes insistent for oxygen. Careless lungfuls of air sigh out of me, a melancholy sound. I am alone in my boredom, isolated by my indifference to everything. I am empty. There is no direction to my life . . . has there ever been? How did I ever come to think I had talent? Why did I ever think anyone would be interested in what I have to say?

Then, just for the sake of filling up your writing time, switch the narration to third person.

> Edna's bored. She's bored by everything. Anyone can see that. It's gotten into her posture, her facial expressions, her breathing. She's so bored she sometimes forgets to breathe. Then a surging yawn sweeps over her as her body becomes insistent for oxygen. Careless lungfuls of air sigh out of her, a melancholy sound. She is alone in her boredom, isolated by her indifference to everything. She is empty. There is no direction to her life . . . has there ever been? How did she come to think of herself as talented? When did she come to believe that anyone would be interested in what she had to say?

At this point you might want to make the narrative more immediate.

> She looks at the confining walls around her. Even her apartment reflects the boredom that rules her life. That depressing Currier and Ives print on her bedroom wall—given to her by Aunt Sarah twenty years ago—it's the very heart and soul of ennui! She takes the print down and slides it under the bed among the dust bunnies. Then she takes it out again and hangs it back on the wall. She hates that picture but feels obliged to keep it where she can see it, where she *has* to see it.
>
> Claude calls to her from the kitchen. "The omelets are just about ready, dear!"

Does Edna interest you? If so, give her some physical properties, describe her. To describe her you have to visualize her first. Is she tall, short, thin, chunky, blonde, pale, nearsighted, nervous, carelessly dressed, well dressed, naked? Does she have small hands white as porcelain? Does she have a jutting chin or a receding chin?

Is her skin smooth, almost poreless, or has it thickened and sagged over the years? Is that a tattoo on her ankle? Why did she paint her toenails green? How about her teeth? Is there lipstick on them? Are they dazzling? Is the upper left bicuspid missing? Does she have a toothache? What's that look in her pale blue eyes? Sorrow? Remorse? Pathological distraction?

Now let's look into Edna's inner state of being. Is she happy? Morose? Bewildered by a sudden change in her life situation? Does she think she is privileged, or does she think life has given her a raw deal? Why doesn't she go with her impulse to bury the Currier and Ives print under her bed? Why does she feel obliged to keep the print where she can see it?

Do you need to put in this much detail? Of course not. Two or three telling characteristics at one time are more than enough. (Chekhov: "Description should be very brief and have an incidental nature.") But whether or not you include any or all of these characteristics in your story, you should have a complete picture of Edna *in your head*. You should know Edna as well as you know yourself. Maybe better than you know yourself—it's easier (and less punishing) to put a fictive character on the dissecting table than your own bundle of sensitivities.

And who is this omelet maker, Claude? Her husband? Her boyfriend? Her gardener? Her psychiatrist? Whoever he is, he might be a character you can rely on to propel the story forward after you write a few more sentences.

Pick and choose. Stored in your memory is a wealth of character types. You've seen them all—at supermarkets, in school, at church, at family reunions, in subways, in buses, and in airports. Whether you realize it or not, you're carrying a vast population of human beings around with you. The older you get, the more you carry. This population is a primary resource. Commune with these folks. Call them into your presence. Use them with élan, humility, compassion, humor, and even ruthlessness.

Maybe by the time you get to Claude and his omelet, you've gotten rid of the boredom idea. Maybe now you've got an idea about Edna and Claude and can begin the story again (now in past tense because you like it better that way).

> Claude called Edna from the kitchen. "The omelets are just about ready, dear!"
>
> Edna took the Currier and Ives prints down from the bedroom wall and hid them under the bed among the dust bunnies. She hated those damn pictures, Claude's favorites. There was something smug about them, smug and stagnant. She felt the same way about omelets. She was beginning to feel the same way about Claude.

Maybe you don't see anything salvageable in this little exercise. That's okay. It's *exercise*. You've had your morning workout. You need to exercise the writing muscle. (It's the long stringy one that runs from your fingertips, up your arms and neck, and into the brain.) Writing, like all physical processes, from calisthenics to juggling flaming torches, takes regular practice. You are training a very special muscle.

The next time you do this exercise you might see a crack of light in a doorway. Go for it. Kick that door open. Get the words *down*.

Have Faith

Give yourself a daily goal of a thousand words, whatever the result. You've got to do this. You can't wait for lightning to strike out of blank blue air. You're lucky when it does, but if you're going to depend on luck, you're never going to get the work done.

If you think you have "writer's block" (a fraudulent term if there ever was one), then do what poet William Stafford suggests: *Lower your standards*. Very often beginning writers (and sometimes experienced writers) find themselves stymied by a need to write with nothing less than journeyman brilliance. They've read the classics, they've read their famous contemporaries, and now they find themselves attempting to do what these others have done so memorably. This is an unreasonable expectation. It can stop the novice cold.

I think a lot of people who have gotten their Ph.D.'s in literature would like to write some literature of their own. But because they know quality when they see it, they can't abide the lackluster prose of their fledgling attempts, and so they quit.

Here's the ugly truth: No matter what your level of literary education, you've got to write tens of thousands of words before you begin to see improvement. Your first efforts (unless you are that rare exception, The Natural Born Writer) are going to be flawed in one way or another. You need to be able to live with this condition. You need to have faith that your work will improve.

Exercise

A writing teacher I know gives this exercise to his students: "Write the very worst story you can think of." It sounds like a bad idea at first. But think about it: This exercise takes a great burden off the beginner. It's asking for mediocrity and worse. It's telling the beginner to forget Melville, Joyce, Woolf, Hemingway, Fitzgerald, as well as all the fine writers working today. It says, "Wallow in the trash heap. Have some low-down messy fun."

In asking the student to write below his or her ability, the student is freed of the responsibility to produce Literature. That's a very good thing to be free of. Anyone who sets out to write Literature is in deep trouble on page one.

Example

The fat yellow moon sat on the horizon illuminating the greasewood bushes between me and that idiot Elrod Tullip. I held my 12 gauge double-barrel duck gun ready. It was going to be him or me, and I had no intention of it being me. First of all, if I really *had* run off with his wife, why would I still be here at the ranch? Why wouldn't I have headed south, across the Rio Grande? And secondly, why would anyone want to run off with Big Hilda Tullip, the chuckwagon cook? Everyone around here knows she gave Elrod ulcers. And I don't mean from her cooking. Not that he didn't deserve every one of those bleeding pinholes in his belly.

"There he is!" Big Hilda hissed, yanking my shirt so hard it came out of my pants. "Shoot the bugger! *Gut*-shoot him!"

And so on.

This is fun because you have no responsibilities to The Body of World Literature. Your only responsibility is to enjoy yourself creating a Punch-and-Judy show on paper.

What does this exercise teach? It teaches spontaneity. It shows how nice it feels to have the words flow swiftly and surely. It also teaches an interesting lesson: Though you set out to write badly, you end up writing at your own level. Once you become interested in the "trash" you're generating, you suddenly begin to bear down. You find yourself working to make the language acceptable and the characters believable.

Try it. See what happens.

End of pep talk. There will be no others.

3

BEGINNINGS, ENDINGS, AND THE STUFF IN BETWEEN

Let me tell you something you already know: A story is an organic whole. It's misleading to talk about a story as if it has distinct inorganic parts that are somehow independent of each other. If I talk about beginnings, I am simultaneously talking about endings and all that happens in between. A story is a living creature, from head to tail. Dissection in the interests of scientific analysis is lethal. You don't assemble it as if it came out of a box and all you have to do is fit the various organs together and apply a little narrative glue. There is no such thing as a story kit.

Even so, every story begins and ends. "Once upon a time" is the archetypal opening just as "They lived happily ever after" is the archetypal exit.

Here are some modern adaptations of the opening.

> Myra straightened herself in the back seat and smoothed her skirt, pushing Jack's hand away.
>
> "All right, baby," he whispered, smiling, "take it easy."
>
> "You take it easy, Jack," she told him. "I mean it, now."
>
> His hand yielded, limp, but his arm stayed indolently around her shoulders. Myra ignored him and stared out the window. It was early Sunday evening, late in December, and the Long Island streets looked stale; dirty white

snow lay shriveled on the sidewalk, and cardboard images of Santa Claus leered out of closed liquor stores.

—"No Pain Whatsoever" by Richard Yates

She flicked her wrist neatly out of Doctor Harry's pudgy careful fingers and pulled the sheet up to her chin. The brat ought to be in knee breeches. Doctoring around the country with spectacles on his nose! "Get along now, take your school books and go. There's nothing wrong with me."

—"The Jilting of Granny Weatherall"
by Katherine Anne Porter

"You're a real one for opening your mouth in the first place," Itzie said. "What do you open your mouth all the time for?"

"I didn't bring it up, Itz, I didn't," Ozzie said.

"What do you care about Jesus Christ for anyway?"

"I didn't bring up Jesus Christ. He did. I didn't even know what he was talking about. Jesus is historical, he kept saying. Jesus is historical." Ozzie mimicked the monumental voice of Rabbi Binder.

—"The Conversion of the Jews" by Philip Roth

That was the fall when the leaves stayed green so long. We had a drouth in August and the ponds were dry and the watercourse shrunken. Then in September heavy rains came. Things greened up. It looked like winter was never coming.

—"The Last Day in the Field" by Caroline Gordon

All these openings have something in common with each other and with the openings of most short stories written in the modern era of short story writing: They drop the reader into a situation that has a history. The history propels the story, and the story either ends the history or starts a new history. In some cases, the story makes it clear that the history is inescapable no matter what the character who owns it does, and that nothing short of death is going to modify or end it.

The opening of the Richard Yates story, through images and dialogue, creates a sordid impression that prepares us for the depressing story that follows. It's a brisk, energetic beginning that drops the reader directly into the action. The history of the central character, Myra, is sketchy. We know she has a terminally ill husband, and that she's about to visit him. Next to her in the backseat of the car is her lover, a sulking groper of doubtful worth.

In the Katherine Anne Porter story, Granny Weatherall, though on her deathbed, cannot escape the pain and humiliation of having been jilted at the altar sixty-odd years in the past. Only her death unties the knot of resentment that has shaped much of her life. She cannot alter her history; she can only escape it.

Ozzie's relentless questioning of theological precepts, in the Philip Roth story, begins after a session of religious schooling at his synagogue. Thirteen-year-old Ozzie has the dogma-demolishing mind of a logician. It seems as if the story is going to be light comedy, but it ultimately deals with the serious consequences of religious doubt. We enter the story at a point in Ozzie's life where his history is going to veer off in a direction his mother and rabbi could never have anticipated and which will appall them.

The first three of the above stories begin with a dramatic flourish. The Caroline Gordon story, however, opens with an almost casual description of nature. We are not dropped abruptly into the middle of the story, but invited into it. The late arrival of fall, however, is emblematic of the narrator's situation, a man with a long history of bird hunting behind him. He is in the autumn of his life, but he is not so old that he can't go out in the field one last time.

All of these story openings capture the reader's interest immediately. In each case, something has happened and something new is about to happen. The reader can't resist the urge to learn more. And this, of course, is the point. A good beginning locks the reader in.

BE A GOOD BLIND DATE

Here's a famous opening sentence.

> It was now lunch time and they were all sitting under the double green fly of the dining tent pretending that nothing had happened.

This is how Hemingway's "The Short Happy Life of Francis Macomber" begins. It's a simple sentence, but look what it does. It drops the reader into a world that requires dining tents with double green flies. It tells the reader that among the several people sitting down to lunch, something has happened, something so unmentionable that the diners are pretending the thing had not happened at all. That's an awful lot for twenty-four simple words to accomplish. We can all learn from the economic majesty of this opening. Look how easily it could go wrong in the hands of a writer who has no sense of the power of economy.

> They were very famished from a long day tramping through the savanna hunting lions. The big lunch tent had already been set up by the bearers and they all went inside and sat down to eat a simple meal of boiled rice, tomato slices, and the center loin roasts from the eland they'd killed the day before. They were more or less silent as they ate. Two of the bearers swatted at flies. No one really wanted to talk about the day's disastrous events.

In using more than three times as many words, the writer of this paragraph has managed to dull the edge of the original opening. The lesson in economy Hemingway teaches is clear: Say everything that needs to be said in as few words as possible.

A story's opening makes this bold promise to the reader: Here follow events of real interest. Keep reading. You won't be disappointed. Kurt Vonnegut once said, "Be a good blind date." (The reader is dating you, the writer, *blind*. Don't be a bore.)

An enticing opening used to be called (and sometimes still is) a narrative hook. Correspondence courses in commercial short story writing asked you to put this sort of verbal gaff into the reader. The advice was given purely for the purpose of catching the eye of an editor so that he or she would read further rather than reject it out of hand. If a skeptical editor was hooked (all editors are skeptical), and if the story was written well enough, the story would sell. The narrative hook was a contrivance, a trick, important only for its power to snag attention. It introduced the story of course, but the lure was obviously just that—a lure.

Here's an example.

> Big Jack Corrigan pulled the arrow out of his thigh and spurred his horse toward the Missouri River where the flatboat would take him all the way to St. Louis and the waiting arms of the buxom Sarah Purcell—unless Crazy Horse and his band of Sioux had other plans for him.

This is shameless beyond apology, but look at this less obvious opening from a 1949 *Redbook* story.

> She told him when the night was held in silence and embers of the moonlight were in the room. He'd understood from her manner while they got ready for bed that she had something special to say, but he did not seem prepared by anything within himself of joy or spontaneity, for what she actually told him: "Darling," she said, hushed as the dark was around them; "darling, I saw the doctor today. It's certain. I'm going to have a baby."

The writing seems a bit precious, but aside from that, you can feel yourself being set up. If this paragraph were a fishing lure, a smart trout would dive for deep water at first sight of its glitter.

This opening on the other hand, is no contrivance.

> The Farquars had been childless for years when little Teddy was born; and they were touched by the pleasure of their servants, who brought presents of fowls and eggs and flowers to the homestead when they came to rejoice over the baby, exclaiming with delight over his downy golden

head and his blue eyes. They congratulated Mrs. Farquar
as if she had achieved a very great thing, and she felt that
she had—her smile for the lingering, admiring natives was
warm and grateful.

This is how "No Witchcraft for Sale" begins, one of Doris
Lessing's *African Stories*. Her opening doesn't strain to capture the
reader's interest. It establishes character and setting and implies a
condition of life in which servants and those who employ them are
the norm. What compels you to continue reading is the self-
confident prose, prose that the reader knows instinctively will be
rewarding.

Am I splitting hairs here? A little. I like strong openings myself.
The thing is, the sophisticated reader does not want to feel manipu-
lated. (Believe me, today's readers of the short story are very sophisticated.) And the brazen narrative hook is manipulative. Is that
always bad? No, not if the writer respects the reader's intelligence
and does not strain to be coy.

This is from James Joyce's "Grace":

> Two gentlemen who were in the lavatory at the time tried
> to lift him up: but he was quite helpless. He lay curled up
> at the foot of the stairs down which he had fallen. They
> succeeded in turning him over. His hat had rolled a few
> yards away and his clothes were smeared with the filth and
> ooze of the floor on which he had lain, face downwards.
> His eyes were closed and he breathed with a grunting noise.
> A thin stream of blood trickled from the corner of his
> mouth.

You could characterize this opening paragraph as a narrative
hook: It has strong attention-getting qualities. However, it introduces, *in the best possible way*, Tom Kernan, the devoted alcoholic.
It certainly is not coy. The fiercely illuminated spectacle of Kernan's
drunk and battered condition continues on for several more pages.
We are made to understand from the start that Kernan is probably
unreformable.

Again, we enter a story that has a history. In this case, we enter at a low point in Tom Kernan's life. Unlike the novel, which has ample time to build a history of the central character or characters, the short story lifts the window blinds on someone's life, then, after we've seen enough to understand something about that life, the blinds are closed. We become momentary witnesses.

GETTING PAST THE BEGINNING

It's important to remember that no matter how well crafted a beginning might be, the writer probably didn't get it exactly right until a first draft of the story had been completed. Unless you know from the outset what your story is going to be about, you can't expect your first-draft beginning to hold up. Most writers *don't* know with undeviating certitude what their stories are going to be about before they've produced drafts. A story is discovered as it is written, even if the writer is able to hold closely to the original inspiration for it. Things are going to occur to the writer in the act of composition that were not in his or her mind early on. The beginning, once the story is fully realized in the mind of the writer, can then be made to correctly herald the story's subject.

Sometimes you will only have a character or two and a dramatic situation in mind. You don't know what's going to happen to them or why. Or maybe you have a sketchy idea of what lies ahead. In either case, start writing. Begin with a flourish. Be bold. Be whatever the initiating impulse wants you to be. Challenge yourself with a fine opening sentence. Then follow it with another. Then a third, and so on until you either throw in the towel or, by gradual accretion, make a beginning. Your ideas will grow, they will change, and new ones will strike out of nowhere like thunderbolts.

I usually don't know what the story is about and don't want to know. I wallow in confusion, misdirection, and eccentric impulse, but I *expect* to find some meaning and purpose as I go along.

I like to read the story as I write it. I like to watch situations and characters emerge, fill out, and develop. And all this happens at the keyboard in flagrante delicto. It's the only chance I'll have to "read" the story fresh. After countless rewrites, the thing will get stale even as it gets better. No help for that. I'll have a general idea of what I'm dealing with—who my characters are and what might happen to them—but beyond that, I'm feeling my way in the dark. I've always liked something E.L. Doctorow said about novel writing: "It's like driving at night. You can only see as far as your headlights, but you can drive across the entire country that way." This applies to short stories, too.

Doctorow is in good company:

> Interviewer: Do you know what's going to happen when you write a story?
>
> Hemingway: Almost never. I start to make it up and have happen what would have to happen as it goes along.

The alternative to this method of composition is to have the story full-blown in your head before you sit down to write it. I know some writers who can do this. I think they are rare birds. If I felt compelled to know the story, beginning to end, before I sat down to write it, I'd choke. And if I didn't choke, I'd be bored. I'd also have a hard time making myself believe the result was all it could have been had I given it time to grow. Furthermore, I'd be giving up the thrill of accidental discovery, the joy of serendipity. A writer "thinks" with his or her pencil or keyboard. As the old lady, quoted by E.M. Forster, said, "How do I know what I think til I see what I say?" My own opinion is this: Why bother to write it if you already know it? It would be, as Gertrude Stein said, like taking dictation.

There's no need to assume the story must be written in one or two sessions. It can evolve over days and weeks, sometimes months. Let the unconscious feed it. Don't be in a big rush. The synchronicities of your world can contribute to it. A good story selectively gathers things to itself from sources that are outside the writer's conscious efforts. The interfering ego is set aside.

Listen to what Flannery O'Connor has to say about the composition of her famous story "Good Country People."

I doubt myself if many writers know what they are going to do when they start out. When I started writing that story, I didn't know there was going to be a Ph.D. with a wooden leg in it. I merely found myself one morning writing a description of two women that I knew something about, and before I realized it, I had equipped one of them with a daughter with a wooden leg. As the story progressed, I brought in the Bible salesman, but I had no idea what I was going to do with him. I didn't know he was going to steal that wooden leg until ten or twelve lines before he did it, but when I found out that this was what was going to happen, I realized that it was inevitable. This is a story that produces a shock for the reader, and I think one reason for this is that it produced a shock for the writer.

Raymond Carver had an interesting response to O'Connor's confession:

When I read this some years ago, it came as a shock that she, or anyone for that matter, wrote stories in this fashion. I thought this was my uncomfortable secret, and I was a little uneasy with it. For sure I thought this way of working on a short story somehow revealed my own shortcomings. I remember being tremendously heartened by reading what she had to say on the subject.

In an interview, the playwright Harold Pinter reveals that he, too, develops the story as he writes it:

I don't know what kind of characters my plays will have until . . . well, until they *are*. Until they indicate to me what they are. I don't conceptualize in any way. Once I've got the clues, I follow them—that's my job, really, to follow the clues.

Robert Frost puts it succinctly.

No surprise for the writer, no surprise for the reader.

Perhaps all this suggests that "the story" *already exists* in some area of the mind that is accessible only when the fingers move over a keyboard. What an appealing (maybe, to some, *appalling*) idea. True or not, I like it. It makes me think that I'm not alone, that my conscious mind—fickle, lazy, and uncooperatively blank, as it often is—is not my only asset. If this is so, then maybe each of us contains thousands of proto stories that exist in the unconscious as arche-types. All we need is a mechanism to draw them up to the surface and the life experiences to particularize them.

Raymond Carver addressed this subject with the following.

> I once sat down to write what turned out to be a pretty good story, though only the first sentence of the story had offered itself to me when I began it. For several days I'd been going around with this sentence in my head: "He was running the vacuum cleaner when the telephone rang." I knew a story was there and that it wanted telling. I felt it in my bones, that a story belonged with that beginning. . . . I sat down one morning and wrote the first sentence, and the other sentences promptly began to attach themselves. I made the story . . . one line and then the next.

JUMP-START THE STORY

I have often contended that fiction writing is more a physical exer-cise than it is an intellectual one. Just as in any sport—shooting baskets, swinging at baseballs, or driving golf balls down a fair-way—the more you do it, the better you get. You can't play good golf by just thinking about your backswing and follow-through. Neither can you write good stories by thinking wonderful thoughts about them. In fact, the more you think about a story, the more it wants to be thought about. It may never get written. You need to put the words down on paper and let them lead you where they will. And more often than not, the story you come up with will bear little resemblance to the story you'd been thinking about.

The French poet Mallarmé said, "Give the initiative to the words." Good advice.

Over the years I've cooked up some exercises designed to jump-start a story. They occasionally work. If beginning a story is difficult, it's because the first paragraph or two must in some sense prefigure the entire story. And how can you do this if you don't know yet what the story will be about? Never mind. Dive straight in and hope there's water in the pool.

Exercise

As you sit down to your keyboard or notebook, convince yourself that your aim is not to compose a short story. Instead, write nothing more than a single interesting paragraph with no long-range goal in mind. The requirements of this paragraph are twofold: It must contain an action of some kind, and it must suggest a mystery. (By "mystery" I simply mean that the action itself is not understandable from what we have been given in the paragraph.)

Example

> The old man in the apple-green suit started passing out candy bars to the group of grade school children at the crosswalk directly in front of Lenora Yount's living room window. It was cold outside, and the old man's hands were chapped red from the raw October wind. "I *am* going to call the police this time," Lenora Yount said to her husband, Irv, who was lying on the couch balancing a martini on his forehead.

These three sentences promise something to the reader. There is an action, and there is a mystery. The questions they raise are multiple: Who is the man in the apple-green suit? Why does he give candy to children? Is he simply generous and kind, or is he a pedophile looking for an opportunity? Why does Lenora Yount make it her business to spy on the man? Why isn't Irv Yount at work? Why is he lying on the couch balancing a martini on his forehead? Is Lenora really going to call the police this time, or, as suggested, fail once again?

Chances are good that a story is present in the answer to these questions. Chances are equally good that the paragraph evokes no response in the writer and remains just what it is, an exercise. But what if the point of view is changed?

> Norrie's at the window again. Every time I look up she's opened the drape another inch. What does she see? She sees what she wants to see. Ugly doings in River City. She says she's going to call the cops on him this time. Old Jensen. All he wants to do is make some kids happy, even in cold weather. That's his crime. Hell, the old-timer has been passing out candy to kids every year since I can remember. He gave *me* candy in a blizzard thirty years ago. Norrie watches too much talk-show television. Jerry and Sally and Montel. Thinks most men with time on their hands are sleazoid creeps. She won't call the cops, though. It's me she hates. It's me she wants to put away. With good reason. But you're too late, Norrie.

Sometimes an adjustment like this can alert the writer to possibilities he or she hadn't recognized. Shifting the point of view, and perhaps the tense, might bring the scene into sharper focus or give it a somewhat different emphasis. The first-person voice might have more appeal for the writer. The changed perspective might trigger something that excites the writer's imagination.

When this occurs, write a second paragraph.

> I got up and made myself another martini. I had to face the board of directors in an hour, and my nerves were edgy. "Where's my good wool suit, Lenora?" I said. "I want to wear the camel hair overcoat my father gave me." She didn't hear me. She already had the phone in her hand, calling her mother. Her knuckles were white. We hadn't been intimate for a year. I carried my martini upstairs and got dressed. I hoped Stella Hanratty would be at the meeting.

Exercise

Study this photograph for a few minutes. Answer these questions: Who are these people? Why is the man on the left looking coyly at the woman on the right? Why is the man in the dark suit staring off into space? Is he sulking? Are the women sisters or competitors or both? What's going to happen later in the evening? What happened earlier?

Now write a couple of paragraphs that directly or indirectly raise these questions but do not answer them.

Do you see the purpose of these exercises? I want you to bypass the Controller. The Controller is the part of your ego that needs to know what it's doing. It hates confusion and misdirection; it distrusts eccentric impulse. It's the map reader, schedule planner, and bean counter. It's the skeptic who loves to kill an idea in its infancy by subjecting it to too many reality checks. Its role is protective: It doesn't want you to make a fool of yourself. It doesn't trust the irrational side of your personality. It wants to protect your public image. But the Controller is dumb. It's so dumb it thinks you *have* a public image.

Most ideas in their infancy are flawed, if not downright silly. If the Controller is allowed to prejudge an embryonic idea, the idea

will never be born. You need the Controller, but not in the beginning. In the early stages of composing a story, the Controller needs
to be tied up and put in the shed.

Here's a sample of an exercise I gave myself a few years ago: Two
people are on a bus. One is itching to start a conversation with the
other. He finally breaks the ice. His audience of one feels trapped.

> The big man next to me on the Greyhound said, "Hear
> me out. I've got two things for you to remember. Cost you
> a dollar. You'll want to remember them if you forget every-
> thing else. I'm talking everything—wife, home, kids, God,
> and country."
>
> The seat wasn't big enough for him. Over the miles his
> bulk gradually spilled over the armrest that divided our
> seats, crowding me. He wore a stained blue suit a size too
> small. He smelled like fried meat. He'd been wanting to
> talk since the Tri-Cities, in the middle of Washington State.
> I leaned against the window and turned up my Walkman
> every time he cleared his throat. But now he caught me off
> guard. I woke up from my nap with his head on my shoul-
> der. We'd napped together like high school sweethearts at
> a midnight drive-in. His long, greasy hair lay on my jacket
> lapels like strands of tarry rope. He spoke in a graveled
> whisper. "I guarantee it—you'll never forget them. Give me
> that dollar and I'll change your life."
>
> "No," I said. "I've got too much to remember as it is."
>
> We passed a school bus full of grade school kids. All of
> them gave us the finger simultaneously.
>
> "Sweethearts," the man said. "Look at those doomed
> sweethearts."

This didn't go anywhere. The men are still on the bus. What the
big man has to tell his reluctant companion remains a mystery, and
the brats are still waving their scurrilous middle digits. I wrote a
similar story later, and that may have satisfied the impulse. I guess
these two are going to spend eternity together in the eastern
Washington steppe.

My file drawer is packed with aborted and abandoned beginnings like these. Some go as many as twenty pages. If I only knew "how" to write a short story I'd have a gold mine. As F. Scott Fitzgerald said to editor Max Perkins in 1926: "If I knew anything I'd be the best writer in America."

ENDINGS

No one can help you here. An ending takes an act of inspiration. I'm talking to myself. For me, the last lines of a story are the hardest to get right. Why is that? I think it's because the ending has to illuminate—perhaps in a new and sometimes unexpected light—all that has gone before. For me, this moment is the epiphany, a moment of realization. The story's epiphanic moment is usually experienced by a character, but sometimes only the reader receives the illumination. When successfully managed, this illuminating moment gives a short story lasting value.

Closure in short story writing has a similar function to closure in poetry. A poem must have closure or it has weak effect. My poetry writing teacher years ago said the ending of a poem is like a ski jump. There's the long accelerating downhill glide, and then, *whoosh*, you are thrown ballistically into space. You had been firmly fixed to the earth, and now you're not. You're sailing off into the novelty and danger of flight. Is that too much to ask of a poem or story? Not at all. That's exactly what we *must* ask.

Here's a poem by James Wright that illustrates what I mean by this "whoosh" effect.

A Blessing

Just off the highway to Rochester, Minnesota,
Twilight bounds softly forth on the grass.
And the eyes of those two Indian ponies
Darken with kindness.
They have come gladly out of the willows
To welcome my friend and me.

We step over the barbed wire into the pasture
Where they have been grazing all day, alone.
They ripple tensely, they can hardly contain their happiness
That we have come.
They bow shyly as wet swans. They love each other.
There is no loneliness like theirs.
At home once more,
They begin munching the young tufts of spring in the darkness.
I would like to hold the slenderer one in my arms,
For she has walked over to me
And nuzzled my left hand.
She is black and white,
Her mane falls wild on her forehead,
And the light breeze moves me to caress her long ear
That is delicate as the skin over a girl's wrist.
Suddenly I realize
That if I stepped out of my body I would break
Into blossom.

The last three lines are stunning. Up to that point the poem has given us lovely images mixed with sentiment, all very pleasant. Had the poem ended on the lines: "And the light breeze moves me to caress her long ear / That is delicate as the skin over a girl's wrist," it still would have been a fine poem, but not an extraordinary one. The final three lines are completely unexpected, even shocking. They transform the experience from a lovely sentiment to the ecstasy of spiritual seizure. They lift the reader into a new realm. Before those last three lines, the reader might have thought he or she had been reading a nice little poem about the sweetness of horses and the poet's affection for them. Then, like a bolt of lightning, we see the poem's real implication: The poem is not about the sweetness of horses or the poet's momentary roadside infatuation; it's about the communion and expansion of souls. *Whoosh.*

How did the poet come up with those lines? Inspiration. Inspired lines are what you need to close a short story. I wish I could tell you how to acquire inspiration, but I can't. It takes patience, it takes depth of understanding, it even takes luck. You might have to wait a year or more to find the lines that end your story properly. I've waited as long as ten years.

About twenty-five years ago, I wrote a story and sent it to *Esquire*. The fiction editor liked it but thought the ending was not right. He couldn't tell me exactly what was wrong with my ending, and he couldn't, of course, tell me how it should have ended. He just didn't like the way I'd closed it.

I didn't either, but I didn't know why. I wrote a dozen new endings for the story, each one worse than the first. The editor didn't like any of them. So, I sent the story with its original ending to *The Atlantic*. The fiction editor there accepted the story immediately, and it was published a few months later.

Even so, I felt there was something wrong. I thought about the story and its faulty ending off and on for years. Then, after about ten years, it dawned on me. I suddenly understood what my story was about and, consequently, how to close it. Isn't that funny? How ridiculous! It took me *ten years* after its publication to figure out how I should have ended it! Did it matter to me that it had been published in a fine magazine? Not a bit. From my newly enlightened perspective, I was able to write an ending that completed the story in a way that now made sense to me.

Patience. It takes patience. And it takes commitment. I liked that story a lot. I owed it my best effort. I couldn't let it go until I had found its proper conclusion.

Some Successfully Concluded Stories

William Carlos Williams' story "The Use of Force" has one of those electrifying endings that takes the reader into unknown territory—into an awareness of how flimsy the mask of civilization is, how easily it slips off. The story, told in first person, is this: A pediatrician makes a house call. A little girl has a raging fever, and since there has been an epidemic of diphtheria, the doctor has to look at her throat. The girl is uncooperative, and the doting parents are more hindrance than help. She won't open her jaws. This dance goes on for a while. Coaxing and threats don't work. At one point the girl rakes her fingers across the doctor's face, knocking his glasses off. The doctor's frustration mounts. The girl splinters a tongue depressor in her teeth. It's total war. The parents wring their hands and say the wrong things, things that only increase the girl's fury. The doctor is furious with the parents, furious with the child. Yet she must be examined. Two children in the area are already dead of diphtheria. Clearly, force must be used. The narrating voice is the doctor's.

> "Get me a smooth-handled spoon of some sort," I told the mother. "We're going through with this." The child's mouth was already bleeding. Her tongue was cut and she was screaming in wild hysterical shrieks.

And then, thinking he should quit and come back in an hour, he desists. But only for a moment.

> I went at it again. But the worst of it was that I too had got beyond reason. I could have torn the child apart in my own fury and enjoyed it. It was a pleasure to attack her. My face was burning with it.

This revelation comes in the fourth paragraph from the end. It is a climax and epiphany, this realization of the horrible joy he finds in unchecked savagery. The story ends three short paragraphs later. The job gets done. To preserve civilization, the brutal use of force sometimes must be used. It's a fine rationalization, but what the doctor discovers about himself—and about us—is made indelible by Williams' story: We not only have it in us to maim and kill, we have it in us to do it with joy in our hearts when necessity gives us the excuse. *Whoosh.*

In John Cheever's "Torch Song," a woman habitually attaches herself to doomed men—drunks, drug addicts, betrayers, abusers— but nothing fazes her. She remains wholesome, good-natured, healthy. Her friend, the story's point-of-view character, Jack Lorey, sees her intermittently over a period of years.

Here's how the story opens:

> After Jack Lorey had known Joan Harris in New York
> for a few years, he began to think of her as The Widow.
> She always wore black, and he was always given to the
> feeling, by a curious disorder in her apartment, that the
> undertakers had just left.

Indeed, all of her lovers come to bad ends—death by sickness,
death by fire, death by suicide. When Jack is down on his luck and
sick and living in a seedy West Side apartment, she comes to him.
He knows her history well, and it spooks him. Her wholesome good
health now seems preternaturally evil to him. Jack orders her away:

> "What kind of obscenity are you that you can smell sick-
> ness and death the way you do?"

This outburst doesn't bother her in the least:

> She finished her drink and looked at her watch. "I'll see
> you later. I'll come back tonight. You'll feel better then, you
> poor darling."

And this is from the last paragraph of the story:

> Jack emptied the whiskey bottle into the sink. He began
> to dress. He stuffed his dirty clothes into a bag. He was
> trembling and crying with sickness and fear. . . . He emptied
> the ashtray containing his nail parings and cigarette butts into
> the toilet, and swept the floor with a shirt, so that there would
> be no trace of his life, of his body when that lewd and search-
> ing shape of death came there to find him in the evening.

Again, these last lines throw a new (if somewhat crazed) light
on all that has gone on before. Joan Harris, in the eyes of the sick
and possibly dying Jack Lorey, is the Angel of Death.

I do these stories a great disservice, giving them to you in fragments, but I want to show you how wonderfully Williams and
Cheever manage closure.

Here's a story of mine that was a lot of fun to write, but I couldn't make sense of it until I discovered the central character's *modus operandi*: He has needs and he fills those needs in a certain way, and though he generally fails, he confidently repeats his obsessive behavior. Though the collected adventures of Gabe and Antoinette didn't add up to anything at first, it didn't matter to me—I was enjoying their antics. I *trusted* that by the end of the story, I would understand what I had been committing to paper well enough to close it successfuly.

LIFE BETWEEN MEALS

"Dig in!" I'd say, and the silverware would fly! Those were the days. If we saw a nibbler we would always be sure to let him see us unload our heaping forks. Our cheeks would balloon, our nostrils flare, and our eyes would roll with the sheer ecstasy of eating. The nibbler would usually dab his pinched-up mouth with his napkin and wash down his pellet of food with quick sips of water. A sickening tribe of birds, are they not? They make me gag.

We traveled a lot. The first thing we would do in a new town would be to scout the restaurants. And I mean *restaurants*. I do not mean the fast-food slop houses, the so-called "coffee shoppes," or the little neighborhood diners where you eat at considerable risk. Ptomaine, I mean. We gave them grades. A for best, F for dismal failure. Quality and *quantity* first, service second. Atmosphere a distant third. We do not eat the atmosphere.

Now hear this: Are you nervous? Are you thin? Then *eat!* What do you want to be like that for? Eat, sleep, and move your bowels. This is basic. This is life. I have seen too many human skeletons, *nibblers*, nervous as cats, eating that ghastly Jello on lettuce. Their reward? Stubborn stool dry as birdshot, and they sleep in fits.

I speak from experience. I was there. We were thin. "Doctor's orders." Antoinette was down to one hundred and forty pounds, and I teetered at two-twenty. We were a pair of rails. I looked somehow fraudulent in my uniform—no bearing, no authority, no style. A year before I'd been up to three-sixteen and Antoinette was a succulent two-oh-nine. We were a hefty duo, and happy. The famous internist said, "You lose one hundred pounds of that lard, Commodore, or you're sunk. Your heart will not bear the strain." And I believed his claptrap.

Broiled slivers of freshwater fish, naked green salads, fruit cocktails sweetened with something made out of coal tar, unsalted wafers, zwieback, fingers of asparagus without a nice blanket of buttery hollandaise, and, of course, the ever-present Jello on lettuce. We went through hell. We suffered. And for what, I ask.

Our health did not noticeably improve. Personally, I felt worse. I believed my death was imminent. I said, "Antoinette, my love, what is life *for?* Answer me that?"

She just cupped her shrinking breasts and laughed, rather thinly I thought. She called me her "enormous whale baby." But there was a hungry glint sharking the blue waters of her eyes. I whispered heavily into her ear, "Banana nut bread, my darling." I let the syllables roll off my tongue like buttered peas. "Chicken Supreme," I said. "Braised Rabbit à la Provence. Shrimp Mull. Creamed Cod Halifax. Marzipan. Fondant. Marshmallow Mint Bonbons." These were some of her favorites.

I wore her down. "My darling," I said. "I could eat raw and rotting squaw fish, I am so very hungry." But Antoinette wanted to remain faithful to the famous internist. She said, "You are forgetting your promise to doctor, Gabe." And I replied, "I do not care about doctor, Antoinette! I am going to die of misery! This is no way to live!" Eventually I won her over. We gave up on the diet and went back to real food. "We are going to be happy again, darling, I promise you." And for a while it was true.

Now hear this: I am hungry all the time. You may choose

not to believe that. You might find such a statement a trifle on the bizarre side. But it is true. I simply do not stay full. I convert food to energy and bulk very quickly. I might go through a platter of oysters on the half shell, a tureen of minestrone, a tub of Texas hash, a loaf of Irish soda bread, three or four slabs of black bottom pie, ten cups of thick coffee, and do it all over again in a couple of hours, believe what you will.

We were cruising around a pretty little inland town checking out Mexican restaurants. We'd found a lovely little place. But Antoinette had the blues. She said, "God, I just don't know anymore, Commodore." Sometimes she called me Commodore. I found it pleasurable.

Something was eating her. She'd been depressed lately. Chewing, her face would sour. She'd put down her fork. "What is it, my darling?" I'd ask. "The meat not done well enough? The sauce flat? Light? Too sweet? Too tart? No character? No spunk?" She would shake her head, run her tongue over her teeth, lift her large breasts off her stomach as if trying to ease her breathing. "Oh, I don't know, Gabe. It's just me, I think." But this was not a satisfactory explanation.

And now, in Guzman's Authentic Sonoran Cuisine, she was balking at the menu. I ordered for her, which was something I hesitated to do. Ordering, after all, is half the *fun*.

"*Matambre, por favor*," I said to the waiter.

"*Matambre*," said Antoinette, "is not Sonoran."

I looked at the waiter, a blond boy with large pimples on his neck, his nose ring outlined with threads of acne. "She is right, you know," I said.

He shrugged. "Get the chicken enchiladas," he said. "It's the best thing on the menu."

"We can get chicken enchiladas anywhere," I said. "No, we'll try the *matambre*."

In fact, it was wonderful *matambre*. My appetite increased. I ordered the *tostadas estilo*, which were made with pig's feet and beans. Antoinette ate as much as I did, but without evident relish.

We drove down to our condominium on San Diego Bay. I like the view, the great naval fleet, the fine tuna seiners, the pleasure craft. Sitting on our balcony, ten floors above the waterfront, I said, "Come on, Antoinette. Out with it. What's wrong, darling?"

There was a platter of cold tongue slices garnished with pimento olives and sweet gherkins between us. The boy had brought them. Antoinette was playing nervously with her diamonds. I tossed a piece of tongue into the air and caught it in my teeth. A small aircraft carrier was easing into the bay. I picked up the glasses to observe it.

"A," she said, "I have no friends. And, B, life between meals is empty."

I put down the glasses and handed her a cool slice of meat. "We have each other," I suggested. In retrospect, I imagine my tone was peevish.

She took a thoughtful bite of the tongue, but would not meet my eyes. The sun was warm on our large bodies. We liked to sit without our clothing on our little terrace, watching the boats. The boy, Wing, was as discreet as only the Chinese can be.

That night, Antoinette woke up in a thrashing sweat. I turned on the lights. "Feel my heart," she said. I pressed my ear to her sweat-filmed breast. Something wild was walloping around in there.

"Take it easy, darling," I said, ringing for the boy. "Try to relax. Was it a dream?"

I had Wing fix a plate of leftover cold cuts for us. It was 3:00 a.m. I opened a quart of Pilsner. I covered two slices of rye with a nice hot mustard and then laid in the meat.

I heard her gagging in the bathroom. She stayed in there for quite a while. Then she came into the kitchen and sat at the table. Her eyes were red and she smelled sour. "Fix me one of those," she said, looking at me with those direct blue challenging eyes that first attracted me to her four years ago.

"With or without," I said, holding up a jar of *Weinkraut*.

"With," she said, defiantly.

I breathed a sigh of relief. Whatever had troubled her sleep had passed. Or so I believed.

That summer I reached a happy three hundred. I felt good. Antoinette was only one-ninety, but she was coming along fine. When she hits two-hundred, I told myself, look out! Her stomach blows out in front, shoving her loaf-like breasts up high and handsome, the nipples spreading wide like brown saucers, and a gossamer rump so soft and creamy it could melt your heart and bring water to your mouth.

"Come over here, you lovely dumpling!" I'd command, and the walls of our condo would shake. I'd imagine the floor joists sagging, the wall studs splintering, the sheetrock crumbling, the roof tiles slipping off and crashing into the streets below.

By fall I made three-twenty and Antoinette reached two-oh-nine, equaling her previous high. We were never happier. We cavorted like honeymooners and ate like young whales. Dig in! Dig in!

We'd go to one of those smorgasbord places just for the fun of it, the ones that advertise, "All You Can Eat For Ten Dollars!" We loved to watch the manager's face sag as we lined up for seconds and thirds and fourths, on and on.

"Fifteen trips, Antoinette," I'd say, a friendly challenge, and she would sweetly reply, "You are on, Commodore!" And we'd fill and empty our trays fifteen times, *heaped*, while the manager would whimper to his girls and shake his head. Once we cleaned out an establishment's entire supply of veal-stuffed zucchini, which was supposed to be the specialty of the house. The manager was a skinny twerp who kept snapping a towel at flies. He didn't bother us.

Now hear this: Skinny people can't be trusted. A man

who can get along on cottage cheese, pears on lettuce, or chicken salad sans mayo, bears watching. A man who keeps a girl's waistline is probably *sly*. I wouldn't touch one of those female skeletons you see in the ads. Like bedding down with tinker toys. I'd crush her dainty innards, her bones would go like twigs. All of them, the thin ones who are thin by choice, are *nibblers*. We once elected a tribe of fancy nibblers to high office and look where it got us. They make me gag.

Steak and potatoes, hot rolls and butter, cheese sauce and broccoli, stuffed eggplant, black bean soup, honey-glazed ham, Bavarian cream, chocolate butter sponge cake, jelly rolls, doughnuts, cookies, ice cream! Eat, eat, enjoy! Make that table groan. What do you have a mouth with teeth in it for? Whistling and smiling?

Our national flag should be a steaming dressed out turkey with stuffing oozing out on a garnished platter.

We were in a nice restaurant up north. Antoinette had been feeling a little moody again and I thought a change of scene would do her good. She was up to two-twenty, an all-time high, and she never looked better. I was holding steady at three-forty-nine. Everyone has an upper limit, unless there's a problem and your glands explode on you. Then you get the six-hundred pound abnormals, the half-ton shut-ins.

Steak and kidney pie was the specialty of the house. The servings were generous enough, but we ordered, as usual, seconds and thirds. Now, the thing is, we were very serious about eating. We would tuck our napkins in and we would *eat*. No small talk. No stopping for cigarettes. If we spoke at all it was to get the salt, the pepper, butter, soy sauce, and so on. Later, over coffee, we might talk.

We would get down, close to the plate, and we would keep the silverware moving. Lift dip, lift dip, lift dip. The object is to get the food into the stomach.

So I did not hear him when he first said it because I was

occupied in the manner described. Then, when he raised his voice, I said, "Are you addressing me, sir?" He said he was. I dried off my mouth with my napkin and looked at him. I do not like to be interrupted when at table.

"You disgusting goddamn pigs," he said.

He was tall and skinny and had a cowboy-thin face that jutted out with years of lean living. I did not like his looks.

"You people look like you got greased life rafts tied around your necks you're so goddamn sinful fat and slobbery."

Antoinette was still eating but her fork had slowed considerably.

"You supposed to be some kind of fucken sailor?" said the cowboy, sneering at me now and looking back to his table for approval. I sat erect in my chair, removed my napkin from my lap, and gazed coolly at him. "You got near everyone in this restaurant ready to blow chunks, the way you pig down that food, admiral," he said.

"That will be quite enough," I said.

He laughed at me and did something obscene. He threw his cigarette on my plate. Then he went back to his table which greeted him heartily, like a returning hero.

"Now hear this, Antoinette," I said. "We will not stand for this impudence. We have our dignity." Antoinette was white as her napkin and her eyes were teary. She had put her fork down. Her lip was trembling. She touched the sides of her neck with her careful fingertips.

"Life rafts?" she said.

I pushed away from the table and stood up. The skinny cowboy saw me coming but he turned his back deliberately as if I was not someone he should be concerned about. No one takes the fat man seriously.

"I believe this is yours, sir," I said.

I had my plate with me, complete with his dirty cigarette sticking out of my mashed potatoes. He turned slowly and

The Art & Craft of the Short Story

looked at me in an offhanded way. Even his mouth was skinny, the lips like blades.

"What's that, pig face?" he said. The two skinny women and the skinny man who were at his table laughed. They were eating breaded fingerlings of some kind and crackers.

I took the back of his head in my left hand and with my right hand I shoved that plate full of ruined food into his face. His mouth yawned open for air under a smothering gray slick of potatoes and gravy. He was quite surprised by my action. Fat men are not generally regarded as quick, strong, or willing to retaliate. This is a common error. At two-hundred pounds I can barely lift a kitten. At three-forty-nine, I am strong as a bear and quick enough. And, I am more than willing to demand satisfaction from the likes of the skinny cowboy.

He jumped to his feet and began throwing punches at me. But he was wild, hitting only my shoulders and chest which met his fists like sofa cushions. I pushed him off balance and kept pushing him until he was against a wall. Then I leaned, belly first, and the air whistled out of him. Antoinette came over then and pinched his cheek so hard that a welt appeared. He tried to kick me but his legs were about as dangerous as pencils. Behind us, his table was laughing and singing *Anchors Aweigh*.

I took Antoinette on a clothes-buying expedition to cheer her up. That ugly incident had made her blues return stronger than ever. At night she would wake up, filled with gas and sour dreams, gagging.

"These dresses," she said, holding several of the new items up. "They are *circus* tents." We'd bought them at the *Wide Pride* outlets, the only clothing emporiums that carry Mega X sizes. We were in our bedroom. I was in bed watching the morning news. The navy, I was sad to learn, was in full retreat before the budget-cutting demands of several skinny congressmen. They were denying the return of the beautiful battlewagons, calling them "fat missile targets." I made up my mind then and there to send telegrams to our legislators, urging them to bring the great wide-beam navy back. Stop this mindless downsizing. Then a commercial came on, diverting my thoughts. Ham and eggs in a sunny kitchen, whole wheat muffins stacked like shingles, prune Danish, fritters, and the lovely girl was taking potato pancakes out of the pan and carrying them to her smiling husband, a good-sized man of healthy appetite. My mouth watered.

Antoinette threw her new dresses aside and stood before her mirror. "Elephant," she said. She made her reflection jiggle and blur by rising up on her toes and letting her weight come down hard on her heels. The room vibrated. Then she began to prance. But it wasn't for fun. She was mocking herself. "Look at me!" she shouted with false merriment. "The elephant is dancing! Come one, come all!"

I thought she looked good. Lovelier than ever. Her rain barrel thighs roared across my field of vision. Her meal-sack breasts swung. Her dimpled rump seemed to fill the room. I was, quite frankly, aroused. I caught her by the wrist.

"Oh no you don't!" she said. But I pulled her anyway. She came down, off-balance, and the wood slats of the bed cracked. Bang, and the bed came down. The room quaked, and I imagined plaster dust graining the air of the room below. "No, Commodore!" she said. "I told you *no!*"

But the Commodore cannot be denied. "Jumbo lover," I whispered hoarsely into her tangled hair. I pinned her and our tonnage moved the seismographs of Spain.

She poked at her breakfast. I didn't like to see that. "Come, come, cupcake," I said. "What's wrong now?"

She looked at me across the laden table, her keen blue eyes gone soft and waxy. She touched her neck, an unconscious habit which began in the restaurant where I had been forced to discipline the skinny cowboy. I folded a piece of ham in half and speared it. She stabbed a fritter but she did not lift it to her lips. I chewed slowly, waiting. My patience,

I confess, was wearing thin. Finally she put down her fork. I put down mine. "My darling," I began. "Everything is either inside or it is outside. Make no mistake. If it is inside, it is being eaten. If it is outside, then it is either eating or waiting to eat. That is all anyone can say about it. The rest is manure. Things on the outside sooner or later find themselves in the inside. For, you see, everything gets its chance at being on the outside *eating*, or in the inside getting *eaten*. My darling, everything in the wide world is food. Us included. It is so very simple. I don't understand your confusion. We are lucky eaters now, but someday that will change. Dig in, my darling. It is the skinny people of the world who are stuffed to their eyes with illusions."

"We're freaks," she said. She left the table and went into the bathroom, where she retched.

I followed her and stood outside the door. "Are you making yourself vomit deliberately, Antoinette?" I asked. She did not reply. "I cannot sanction that, my darling. I can never sanction that." Still she did not reply. Then I humbled myself. I knelt on both knees before the sullen door. "Ah, love, we *must* be true to one another," I said. "We have nothing else, don't you see?" But she would not answer.

Now hear this: Like most large men I'm tolerant and easy to get along with. But there is a line. If you are a skinny man you may not understand what I am saying here. Suppose, then, that you are a skinny dancer and you have married a skinny woman who is also fond of dancing. Then she decides, without consulting you, that she's tired of dancing and would rather sit down and eat. Soon she blossoms out to a healthy size eighteen or twenty and will not roll back the carpet when the Lawrence Welk re-run comes on TV. You soon begin to feel stupid foxtrotting around your rumpus room with a barstool in your arms while the little woman has her face parked in the Kelvinator. Where is the little girl I married, the girl with the twinkling feet? you ask yourself. I shall tell you where she is. She has shipped out. That size eighteen or twenty with the drumstick in her hand is someone else. You have begun to sense this yourself and have taken to calling her the USS *Tennessee* or some such appellation meant to discourage her. But she is not discouraged. She has, perhaps, found herself a new companion, fat as herself, and you find them together laughing wonderfully between mouthfuls of guacamole dip and tortilla chips. You're beginning to feel left out. You are disgusted by her. You are angry. Bitterness taints every bite of food you take and you grow skinnier and thus even farther away from her than ever. She asks, so innocently, what's wrong with you lately and you can only stare at her as if she is the last person in the world who has the right to ask that question. But you won't say a word because you are afraid, at this point, of what might happen if you open your mouth and let loose what's really troubling you. You have been *betrayed*, skinny, but you cannot say a word because that kind of betrayal is not punishable by God's law or by court martial.

A betrayer needs an ally. Our condominium had a number of candidates. Skinny food-haters, dozens of them. Fifty-year-old business executives with the bodies of school boys. Suntanned grandmothers in string bikinis. You never see them with food in their mouths. They live on vitamin supplements and protein tablets. One of these food-haters, Bessie Carr, gave Antoinette a subversive menu guaranteed to burn away her fat in a matter of weeks.

Antoinette refused to sit down with me and discuss it. "My darling, such diets are dangerous," I said. She looked at me with that challenge in her eyes, but it wasn't the same. There was no promise of fun in this new defiance. I felt sick at heart.

"You are the one, Gabe, who is digging his grave," she said. "And you are digging it with your mouth."

It was the realization of my worst fears. It had happened to me before, with the others. *Am I cursed?* I asked myself. A trichinosis of self-doubt undermined the shank and brisket of my soul.

"Come, my darling," I said one morning, hoping to retrieve something of our former happiness, "let us do a Roly-Poly." But she looked at me with icy disgust. We hadn't done a Roly-Poly since our honeymoon and the two or three months of high excitement that followed. Yes, it is the pinnacle of frivolity, but I was desperate. My life, once again, was listing severely and threatening to capsize.

"Don't be vulgar," she said.

We used to do it in the hot tub. It was a game. We'd get about seven hundred tins of liverwurst and Wing would open them on the electric opener. Then we would cover ourselves with the tasty paste. We would roll and slide in the drained tub, nibbling liverwurst from each other until it was gone. It was the appetizer to afternoons filled with a smorgasbord of delights. I can remember Antoinette rolling like a dolphin and murmuring, "Yummers." Once we tried deviled ham, but it did not hold well to the skin. Those were the days. We were hot pink whales in a soupy bay.

But now her fat was going like lard in a skillet.

I began to eat for both of us, as if I could maintain her bulk by doubling my intake. By the time she dropped to one-fifty, I had climbed to three-eighty. I had passed my upper limit and the difference made me nervous and gassy.

Bessie Carr used to be fat herself. She brought over an album of snapshots showing her progress from a size twenty-two to a size nine. They were at the kitchen table, poring over the pictures. I said, leaning over them, "Now hear this: *there* is a woman after my own heart." I pointed to a picture of Bessie lying in a child's wading pool. Arms and thighs, like great roasts, fell over the sides of the inadequate pool. Her breasts expanded in the buoyancy of water. They looked like fine wheels of white cheese. The pale hummock of her belly was a vast, North African kingdom. She turned the pages, however, until she found herself thin. There she was in a bikini, daylight blaring between her thighs even though she was standing in a normal way.

So much daylight, quite frankly, that you could have placed an entire chicken between her upper thighs and it would have fallen to her feet without touching her! It was horrible, enough to make a leper queasy. I sighed regretfully and they both looked at me with undisguised scorn, and then pity.

"Adipose Tissue and Its Spiritual Implications," said the brochure I happened to find on Antoinette's vanity. I thumbed through it. There was a good deal of nonsense about something called, "The Great Need." It seemed that we were very hungry, but not for food.

I went into the living room to point out the foolishness of such claims to her. She was sitting on the floor, before a black man with thickly lidded eyes. The black man was on the TV set, speaking in low tones. He was wearing a turban of some kind.

"Antoinette," I said. "May I have a word with you?"

"Shh," she said.

"Please, my darling, we must discuss this thing."

She turned to me then, annoyed. "I am listening to Sri Raj," she said sharply.

"I would rather that you listened to *me* for a moment," I said, somewhat offended.

"No," she said. "I'm learning about it."

"It?" I asked, glancing at the black man who seemed on the verge of nodding off to sleep.

"Life, Gabe," she said. "I'm learning how to flower. The spiritual garden within is starving, according to Sri Raj."

I dropped the brochure. It fluttered to the floor beside her. "I'm going to have lunch," I said. "I'd like you to join me, Antoinette." I snapped off the TV set.

This angered her. "Don't call me Antoinette any more!" she said. "My name is Debbie! I've always *hated* that name Antoinette!"

"Have you now," I said.

"Yes, I have! It's a pig's name! Farmers give their eight-hundred pound sows names like Antoinette and Veronica and . . . and . . . *Emmeline!*"

"Do they," I said.

She turned the TV back on and the black man rolled into the screen. "Be joyful, then, as the little birds," he said.

I lunched alone. Wing, sensitive as ever to crisis, had made a wonderful Viennese *linzertorte*, one thousand calories per serving!

"Wing, old son," I said, affectionately. "Pack up my uniforms. I am afraid it's time to ship out."

And ship out I did. I am not such a fool as one who will humiliate himself before the inevitable. I bought into another condominium up the bay toward the city. Of course, I missed her terribly. I always miss them terribly. And why shouldn't I? It is no great pleasure to take your meals alone, is it? And what of the great restaurant hunts? The round-robin eating binges? The king-size bed with double-strength frame? Such a bed needs a great and ample queen.

Faithful Wing drove me about the city, looking for a new companion. Wing's careful manner at the wheel tended to hold my eagerness in check. The way he held to the speed limits, the sober way he lifted the gear lever, the delicate gloved hand on the wheel—all these things served as an example to my hasty mind. Haste, in such a weighty enterprise, can serve no good purpose. Had I taken more time to observe Antoinette four years ago, I might have detected the worm of discontent that eventually fouled our pleasant arrangement.

"I think we should look for a younger one this time, Wing," I said. "One with a simpler, more reliable outlook."

Wing understood immediately and turned the car toward the beach areas where the cheap, fast-food restaurants thrive. We cruised the neon boulevards, scanning.

"Starboard bow, Wing," I said, pointing to a place called *Holy Cow*! It was a hamburger house shaped like Borden's Elsie. Sitting alone on the patio, a tray of giant cheeseburgers before her, was a likely prospect, a hefty redhead of eighteen or so. Her complexion was unfortunate, perhaps, but a year of clean, expensive food properly prepared would clear it up just fine. There were other young people there, but they sat tables away, avoiding her as though she had a dreaded disease.

We sat in the parking lot for half an hour, simply observing her. Wing had the video camera going and I was making copious notes. Even though I was wearing my elegant "King Edward" naval uniform, and would have made a smashing impression on her, we needed to exercise some empirical caution this time. But all the signs looked very good.

The longer I watched her lift those cheeseburgers to her lonely but shameless jaws, the more convinced I was that we were meant for each other. Her name was probably Kathy, Wendy, Jean, or Pam—something that did not give credit to her true nature. I thought about it for a while, then snapped my fingers, making Wing jump.

"Roxanne!" I said. "We shall call her Roxanne!"

Antoinette's gradual disaffection leads to her ultimate betrayal of Gabe. She commits the unspeakable sin: She goes on a diet. She becomes thin. But Gabe, undaunted as an admiral of the sixth fleet, sails confidently on. He patrols the boulevards looking for a new young woman, a prospect who will be likely to share his love of unapologetic gluttony. "Roxanne" we now realize, is the latest in a long chain of young female shipmates for the commodore. And this, for me at least, gave the story the resonance it needed. Now that we understand that Gabe's relationships are serial, and therefore unsuccessful, we can understand the story in that light. We can see the whole saga of binge-eating repeating itself as Gabe and Roxanne tour the restaurants of California. Antoinette had her predecessors, just as she is Roxanne's. It's an unending story.

A sense of timing, a sense of "rightness," the ability to illuminate the human drama you've committed to print. That's all you need to close a story successfully. Good luck to you. Good luck to me.

4
———

THEME VS.
"WHAT MY STORY IS ABOUT"

There is at least one theme embedded in "Life Between Meals."
I'll put on my critic's hat and give you my take on it: Gabe—
in his naval attire, in his insatiable appetite, in his unshakable
conviction that his gluttony is not only justified but something
to be proud of—represents the spirit of unchecked imperialism.
He mourns the demise of the "wide-beam navy"—the necessary
military might to advance an imperialistic cause. The women he
takes up with have been "colonized" in that he makes them over
in his own image—an imposed assimilation akin to the missionary's practice in a colonized territory of converting the natives to
Christianity. Gabe, like any member of the ruling class, has a
faithful third-world servant, Wing, who takes care of all his
needs. His favorite costume is his "King Edward" naval uniform,
a bright emblem of the nineteenth century's imperialist vision.
And so on.

Did I think of all that before I sat down to write the story?
Absolutely not. Had I done so, I'm sure the tale would have been
stiff, predictable, and heavy-handed. I would have distracted myself from the job of storytelling by looking for opportunities to
make my point rather than allowing the characters the freedom
to act consistently. If there was a thematic point to be made, it
would have to emerge organically from the natural interaction
of the characters.

MULTIPLE THEMES

I can look at "Life Between Meals" from different critical perspectives, each of which yield other but equally plausible themes.

A Freudian critic might see Gabe as a man whose psychosexual development has been arrested in the oral stage of emotional growth. Indeed, Gabe is rather childlike in his attitudes and desires, and his primary form of gratification is the ingestion of large volumes of food. Again, if I had started out with this in mind, I would have seized every opportunity to "prove" the point. The story would have been packed with symbols consistent with analytical psychology. There probably are such symbols in the story, but they occur naturally and were not employed in the interests of a particular scheme.

A critic coming to the story from a feminist viewpoint would no doubt see Antoinette as a woman surrendering her selfhood to a patriarchal society that requires this sacrifice. Her subsequent rebellion is the historical rebellion of women who have rejected the traditional roles imposed on them. This view of the story is incontestable. But was that in my mind as I wrote? I confess, it was not. Again, had this been a primary consideration, the story would have been restricted in ways it now is not.

A critic coming to the story from a mythological standpoint might see Gabe as a Dionysian character, Antoinette as a reluctant and timid Psyche, and the tale itself as a saturnalia of excess.

If the American Dietitian Association decided to venture into literary criticism, it would understand "Life Between Meals" as a dire commentary on the American compulsion to overeat, the tragedy of obesity, and the dangers of the high-fat low-fiber diet. "The Commodore's suicidal ingestion of high-cholesterol foods is indicative of our national love affair with fast-food establishments," such a critic might write.

There are as many themes in a story as there are critical theories. But the term "theme" is part of the critic's vocabulary, not the writer's. You wouldn't think so if you took a class in literature at most universities. Very often, literature is taught in a way that gives the writer credit for understanding all the implications of his or her work. This is flattering to the writer, but it's wrong.

If a piece of writing has any depth at all, it's going to reverberate with meanings the writer was never conscious of. It's the critic's job to discover these. The fact that the writer didn't consciously intend those meanings doesn't invalidate them. Done well, criticism illuminates a work in such a way as to give it greater accessibility.

I once wrote a short novel based on the Frankenstein idea. *A Lovely Monster* takes place in contemporary California. A university microbiologist "builds" a human being from the body parts of others. As the first draft progressed, the notion of what the story was about took shape: My "monster" would be more human than the man who created him and the people who subsequently exploit him. It's the idea behind King Kong, too. That was it. Nothing more than that simple idea ever presented itself to me.

A friend of mine read the novel. He asked if I'd had in mind the notion that, as Americans, we are really the stitched-together fragments of many nationalities. Had I intended my "monster" to represent the genetic and cultural diversity of the typical American? I had to answer no. It never occurred to me. But my friend's idea is valid. It makes sense. There are no doubt other thematic ideas present in that novel, ideas I would never have thought of on my own. And that's okay. It's an unavoidable feature of language and of the art of story writing. Our language is public property—anyone is free to make deductions and inferences from a work constructed of language.

Here's what I'm getting at: Don't analyze a work in progress for its deepest meanings. Don't think of your work as having a major theme before you've produced a draft. You might hamstring your imagination if you do. Remember this: *You don't begin with meaning, you end with it.*

Katherine Anne Porter, speaking of her story "Flowering Judas," said, "I named it 'Flowering Judas' after it was written, because when reading back over it I suddenly saw the whole symbolic plan and pattern of which I was totally unconscious while I was writing."

Rita Mae Brown, in her book *Starting From Scratch*, says,

" . . . theme must come from within you. If it doesn't, you're nothing more than a hired gun. You won't be writing true fiction. It may be fictional in form but it won't be fictional in intent. . . . True fiction is always lived from within and deeply felt."

AN ORGANIZING PRINCIPLE

So don't concern yourself with theme. All you have to be able to do is to tell yourself, at some point in a story's composition, what the story is *about*. Telling yourself "What the Story Is About" is a far less intimidating notion than stating its theme. "What the Story Is About" is an organizing principle, a road map that keeps you from straying into "What the Story Is *Not* About."

When I completed the first draft of "Life Between Meals," I knew my story was about a very large gluttonous man with eccentric habits who has an equally gluttonous female companion who eventually walks out leaving him to seek a new gluttonous female companion. That's it. Nothing more. All that stuff about imperialism occurred to me long after the final draft had been completed. Then and only then could I play at being a literary analyst, and only for my own amusement.

Let me give you an example of what I'm talking about.

Say you want to write a story about the abhorrent conditions illegal migrant workers have to suffer at the hands of the *coyotes* who transport them across the Mexico-U.S. border. Your initial idea is to expose a great social wrong. You might begin to think of this as your theme.

You've done the research required. You've read articles about groups of illegals who have died in the deserts of Arizona, New Mexico, or west Texas, locked in the backs of semitrailers, abandoned by the *coyote* who has their passage money in his pocket. You've driven to the southwest deserts in August to sample the cruel heat firsthand. Perhaps you've interviewed a few men and women who have been transported across the border illegally. Your sense of outrage is great, and this outrage is, in large part, your motivation. Your sense of theme is building—social injustice, economic inequities, man's inhumanity to man, and so on. From the bridge connecting El Paso to Juárez, you've seen the graffito, painted on the Rio Grande's concrete embankment—*Todos somos ilegales* (We are all illegals)—and it touched you.

In your story, the truck, loaded with more than a hundred half-suffocated illegals, stops at a roadside cafe. The *coyote* wants a cool drink. The suffering men inside pry the locked door open a bit to get some air. The outside temperature is 115°. They gulp in the hot air and regain confidence in their future situations north of the Rio Grande. One of the smaller men squeezes out of the narrow opening. He has no faith in the *coyote* and believes that he and his companions are being led to their deaths. He's heard rumors that once they have their money, some of the *coyotes* never deliver the men to the jobs that are supposed to be waiting for them in the United States, and that the so-called jobs are fictions. He believes the men will be left to die in the desert. The man who has managed to get out of the truck tries to persuade others to join him, to convince them that their chances would be better if they went on foot. But the men don't agree. Their families back in Mexico will be destitute unless they get the jobs promised to them. The man considers the situation. His friends are in the truck. Can he abandon them? He makes his choice: Though he knows the *coyote* will bolt the door shut again, *he gets back in.*

End of story.

But what is it about? The major themes of injustice, social inequity, man's inhumanity to man? No, not any longer. These are now the backdrop for another drama, a drama you hadn't set out to portray, a drama that emerged as you wrote. Somewhere in the composition of your first draft something surprising happened— you were inspired by a gesture you hadn't envisioned when you started writing: The man who wanted to leave the *coyote* gets back in the truck, even though he believes it might cost him his life. The story now is about *that*. Now, if you want to assign a theme to it you can. You can safely say the story's theme is brotherhood: the unbreakable ties that bind one man to another. The plight of migrant workers in the hands of the often ruthless men who transport them, and the social conditions that have given rise to it, is now the context for a story about a brave migrant worker who gets back into the doomed truck though he knows the possible consequences of doing so.

Had you been rigidly committed to the instigating "theme," you might have written with tunnel vision and the heart of the story that finally gets told would have been missed.

You don't begin with meaning, you end with it.

5

CHARACTERS

The short story is a modern adaptation of the older forms, drama and poetry. If it has any power at all, it is because it honors these aesthetic roots. Like the poet, the short story writer must always be conscious of word selection, as well as the rhythms produced by aggregations of words. The short story writer must have—or at least try to develop—an ear for the language. This is the poet's primary concern. Atonalities, discordances, unintended repetitions must be detected and the offending phrases rooted out and rewritten.

The drama's great advantage over the short story is the live presentation of characters, on stage, before the witnessing audience. The audience sees them in the flesh, hears them speak their lines, believes implicitly in their reality. Suspension of disbelief is relatively easy for the dramatist. The stage is set, the characters are there—what's not to believe? (Of course, bad writing and poor direction can turn flesh-and-blood actors into talking crash dummies.) But the short story writer has to convince the audience that the characters assembled on the page are as solid and three-dimensional as they would appear on a stage.

The stage the short story writer is dealing with is the reader's mind. Somehow, these little black squiggles against a white background, these phonetic symbols we call written language, must make manifest in the mind of an indifferent reader a world of dimension, sound, and color, occupied by actual people. When you think of it, it seems a real miracle that this ever occurs. These black squiggles represent nothing more than sound. And the collection of sounds they make produces meaning. *The sounds in a sentence can produce three-dimensional holographic images in the mind.* I find that astonishing. I also find it intimidating. What an art this is that can, out of scratches on a page, evoke an inhabited world.

Nothing is evoked, though, if the characters have nothing but expected qualities, no unexpected ones, that is, if they are no more than stereotypes, as in the following example:

> Sylvia Merchant was a beautiful woman. Even the most indifferent and casual glance would prove this true to the most nonchalant observer. She was tall and willowy, and blessed with the natural dignity one usually associates with the aristocracy. Though she occupied a prominent niche in Slocum Falls society, she hoped beyond reason that, by now, she'd earned a niche in Lyle Nickerson's heart. After all, he had brought her through some very difficult times. She looked forward to these sessions and hoped that he did too. When she thought of his command of his subject matter, his subtle yet forceful technique, and how she had benefited so greatly from it, she felt exalted and yet humble. She entered his pleasant, upscale apartment upon his suave, "*Entrez-vous, cheri*," and heaved a sigh. Her face was flushed with excitement, yet she was stricken with that old recurring self-doubt. *Is it me, or is it my potential he admires so?* she thought to herself.
>
> Lyle, handsome in an unconventional way, yet flawed—which only made him seem all the more mysterious—was wearing his velvet smoking jacket. His chiseled visage was dimly illuminated by the fading crepuscular light of late autumn which beamed its declining seasonal rays weakly through the large bay window directly behind his concert-size grand piano. "So," he said, his voice sonorous, and fulsome, perhaps, with as yet unexpressed desires, "you've come at last, Sylvia."

"Yes, I have," Sylvia half-whispered.

"I knew you would," Lyle replied, indifferently.

After an awkward moment, Sylvia confessed, "I don't think I can go on with it, Lyle."

"But my *dear*—"

"Oh, it isn't you. You've been so very gracious and understanding. It's me. I don't think I have the emotional resources to make a long-term commitment."

Lyle regarded her for a moment. He cupped his chin in his hand thoughtfully, reassessing his protégé. "Perhaps you do not," he said at last.

This is wretched writing. (I hear you—you've seen published work that isn't a whole lot better. But the ever-popular hot dog is full of the abattoir's floor sweepings, too.) It's wretched because of the following:

1. The description is either non-existent or abstract: Lyle might be giving her piano lessons, T'ai Chi instruction, or high colonics, there's no way to know. "Handsome" and "beautiful" without help from specifics ("unconventional" describes nothing) are meaningless. And what *is* a "pleasant, upscale apartment"? It is whatever the reader wants it to be since the writer doesn't seem to care.

2. The piece is full of clichés: Almost every line contains one.

3. It's redundant: That "crepuscular light" is tweaked to death by at least five modifiers that say much the same thing.

4. The bloated diction is both elevated and stupid (a good trick!), creating an instant sense of unreality.

5. Worst of all, these characters are dead on page one. No resuscitation is possible. Their dialogue is stiff, stuffy, and unrevealing.

This is no way to introduce characters, and certainly no way to begin a story.

THE VENTRILOQUIST AT WORK

The contemporary short story, with rare exceptions, is exclusively character driven. This means the action ("plot," if you want to use that term) is generated by the central character's predicament. If the writer hasn't created believable characters, the reader won't care what happens to them. Mother Teresa herself couldn't care what happens to Sylvia Merchant.

What constitutes believability? In first-person narrations the believability issue is almost skirted. The narrator takes the reader by the lapels and says, "Listen, this is what happened to me," or, "This is what I witnessed." The character *is* the voice. If this self-characterization fails, it's not because the tale the narrator tells is far-fetched but because the narrating voice is not consistent. Suppose this narrator starts out with the following line.

> By and large my situation at Fleming Place, though not entirely insufficient to my purposes, was not what I, in my fondest hopes, had expected. . . .

Then the narrator drifts into another pattern of speech.

> This fleabag sucked big time. I told the old hag who ran the dump I wanted a room with a view of the street. But no, she sticks me in a room where the only window looks into an air shaft.

This is extreme, but *any* departure the narrating voice takes will automatically signal the reader that the writer has no firm concept of who the narrator is. When this happens, believability is lost. I see this in student writing all the time. At one point a narrator might take pains, for whatever reason, to avoid contractions.

> I do not drive much at all these days and I will not drive into town on Fridays. The pre-weekend traffic could not be worse, and besides, my driving skills are not what they once were.

Then later in the story, the narrator suddenly slips into a less formal style, employing contractions.

> Jeanne wouldn't buy my version of why she'd been treated badly. I didn't mean to actually lie to her, but I couldn't tell her the raw truth. She wouldn't have understood.

This seems minor, but even seemingly insignificant variations will damage believability.

In "Life Between Meals," the story itself is preposterous, but I think I was careful enough to make Gabe's voice consistent throughout. Had I lost control of the voice, the story would have collapsed under the weight of its extravagance.

Look how Barry Hannah establishes his character in his story "Testimony of Pilot."

> When I was ten, eleven and twelve, I did a good bit of my play in the backyard of a three-story wooden house my father had bought and rented out, his first venture into real estate. We lived right across the street from it, but over here was the place to do your real play. Here there was a harrowed but overgrown garden, a vine-swallowed fence at the back end, and beyond the fence a cornfield which belonged to someone else.

The autobiographical voice is firmly established in this first paragraph. We trust it to remain the same. And it does, even as the drama it tells becomes more complex.

Try another example, this one from John Cheever's "Goodbye, My Brother."

> I don't think about the family much, but when I remember its members and the coast where they lived and the sea salt that I think is in our blood, I am happy to recall that I am a Pommeroy—that I have the nose, the coloring, and the promise of longevity—and that while we are not a distinguished family, we enjoy the illusion, when we are together, that the Pommeroys are unique.

Again, the character-establishing voice is distinctive and reliable.

I don't think of the first-person autobiographical method as me, even if the story really is autobiographical. I like to think of my character as a puppet sitting on my knee: I am the ventriloquist providing the puppet's voice. In the art of ventriloquism, the timbre of the puppet's voice, its manner of speech, the attitudes that establish its persona are everything. Once you successfully invent such a character, believability is automatic.

I probably shouldn't have to emphasize this, but I want you to understand from the outset that in first-person narration, the "I" character is *never* you, the writer, even when you are writing from intimate personal experience. If you've done the job correctly, you've transformed that experience into fiction. And fiction is what *didn't* happen. All else is reportage.

CHARACTERS WITHIN A CHARACTER

When the character narrating the story presents another character, think of this as a character within a character. In "Life Between Meals," Gabe presents Antoinette: We experience Antoinette through Gabe's eyes. He sees her only as a companion in gluttony, a kindred spirit. When she strays, he sees only betrayal. But the reader sees Antoinette as someone trying to find her own identity by abandoning the one that's been imposed on her. Gabe's version of Antoinette is colored by his compulsions and is not reliable.

Is this true for all first-person narrators? Some writers will want you to accept their first-person narrators as completely reliable, keenly objective observers, but even then we need to keep in mind who is presenting these characters and what his or her priorities are. It isn't, after all, a neutrally omniscient narrator—a narrator required to have a strong stake in objectivity—who illuminates these characters for the reader. I'm not saying that a first-person narrator must necessarily give the reader a false version of other characters. I'm only saying that you have to read these characters in context of the narrator's personal history, maturity, intelligence, and biases.

Mary Lavin's story "My Vocation," about a young Irish girl who has a momentary fantasy about becoming a nun, is a case in point. The girl's fantasy is shattered by the visit of a pair of nuns who come to interview her. Here's how she describes them.

> One of them was thin all right, but I didn't like the look
> of her all the same. She didn't look thin in an ordinary way;
> she looked worn away, if you know what I mean? And the
> other one was fat. She was so fat that I was afraid if she
> fell on the stairs she'd start to roll like a ball.

This is our first view of the visiting nuns. Later in the story their superior, inquisitional manner puts the girl permanently off her "vocation." The description of the nuns is not objectively neutral but visceral, imbedded in the language and prejudices of a teenage girl who in truth is more interested in boys than in the religious life. The description serves the story well, and is true in a narrow sense, but it denies the nuns the full range of complexities any human being possesses.

In John Updike's "A&P," the teenage grocery clerk sees two girls who enter the store this way.

> The one that caught my eye first was the one in the plaid
> green two-piece. She was a chunky kid, with a good tan and
> a sweet broad soft-looking can with those two crescents of
> white just under it, where the sun never seems to hit, at the
> top of the backs of her legs.

Here, the focus of this description is hormonally determined. We are seeing the girls through the eyes of the sexually charged high school boy who narrates the story.

Even in a story written in the autobiographical style, where there is a pretense of truth telling, the narrator defines other characters from a singular perspective. My story "Safe Forever" is about a boy whose home life is chaotic. When the boy's stepfather, Dan Sneed, leaves for a job in Texas, the boy's mother, who works in a shipyard in the San Francisco Bay Area, takes up with a fellow shipyard worker who's just been laid off. Here's how the first-person narrator describes the new man in the house.

> His name was Mel Sprinkle. He'd worked in the Kaiser
> shipyards, too, and had yet to find another job that suited
> him. He made me nervous. He hung around the house most

of the day, reading the newspaper and making phone calls. "There's not much work for a man like me," he'd say. I took that to mean either that he was overqualified for most of the jobs he saw advertised or that his skills were rare and generally unappreciated. He was muscular and athletic-looking and he ate everything I cooked, but he didn't seem to have much energy. He wore one of Dan Sneed's old bathrobes around the house while he drank coffee and studied the want ads.

There is nothing inaccurate or misleading about this view of Mel Sprinkle, but it is given by a narrator who has a personal stake in the unfolding action of the domestic drama. The narrator may not come right out and say it, but he clearly finds Mel Sprinkle lacking in admirable qualities. The description is consequently—and necessarily—narrow.

A FEW DEFT STROKES

In third-person stories, the problem is different, and for some writers, more challenging. Here the narrating voice is self-effaced—an absence in the air, a nonentity, a ghost the reader must come to trust. It establishes the reality of the story's central character(s) through an objective rendering that allows the reader to see the three-dimensional being the writer intends the reader to see. (Sometimes in third-person narrations, the objectivity is deliberately compromised. See chapter nine on point of view.) This is most often done with a few deft strokes.

That afternoon all the fellows followed Michael up the ladder to the roof of the old building and they sat with their legs hanging over the edge looking out at the whitecaps on the water. Michael was younger than some of them but he was much bigger, his legs were long, his huge hands dangled awkwardly at his sides and his thick black hair curled up all over his head. "I'll stump you all to jump down," he said suddenly, and without thinking about it, he shoved himself off the roof and fell on the sawdust where he lay rolling around and laughing.

This is from Morley Callaghan's "The Runaway." Callaghan doesn't waste words nailing down the image of young Michael. These few words bring the boy immediately into sharp focus—he's big for his age, gangly, boastful, and impulsive. As the story progresses, we see Michael in other, less heroic, contexts, and by the story's end we know this character intimately.

Look how the careful selection of descriptive words establishes the character of the innkeeper in this excerpt from a V.S. Pritchett story.

> The four men were surprised to see a woman standing behind the door, waiting there as if she had been listening to them. She was a frail, drab woman, not much past thirty, in a white blouse that drooped low over her chest.
>
> "Good morning," said Sid. "This the bar?"
>
> "The bar?" said the woman timidly. She spoke in a flat wondering voice and not in the singsong of this part of the country.
>
> . . . The four men were tall and large beside her in the little room and she gazed up at them as if she feared they would burst its walls.

You not only see this character in "Many Are Disappointed," but you also see *into* her. You see how her inner life is made visible through her physical presence.

Pritchett's word selection is perfect: "She was a *frail, drab* woman, not much past thirty, in a white blouse that *drooped* low over her *chest*." See how different the effect would have been had Pritchett used four words other than the ones I have italicized: "She was a delicate, plain woman, not much past thirty, in a white blouse that fell low over her breasts."

The substitution of "delicate" for "frail," "plain" for "drab," "fell" for "drooped," "breasts" for "chest" establishes her sexuality, while "frail," "drab," "drooped," and "chest" eliminate it (which, of course, is Pritchett's intention), even though the substituted words are close in meaning to the original words. And her "flat wondering voice" sets her apart from the expected warm welcome of an innkeeper. Her timidity is captured wonderfully by the sentence "The four men were tall and large beside her in the little room and she gazed up at them as if she feared they would burst its walls." This is the art of characterization at its best.

Let's see how Carson McCullers works this magic in her story, "Wunderkind."

> She came into the living room, her music satchel plopping against her winter-stockinged legs and her other arm weighted down with school books, and stood for a moment listening to the sounds from the studio. A soft procession of piano chords and the tuning of a violin. Then Mister Bilderbach called out to her in his chunky, guttural tones:
>
> "That you, Bienchen?"
>
> As she jerked off her mittens she saw that her fingers were twitching to the motions of the fugue she had practiced that morning. "Yes," she answered. "It's me."
>
> "I," the voice corrected. "Just a moment."
>
> She could hear Mister Lafkowitz talking—his words spun out in a silky, unintelligible hum. A voice almost like a woman's, she thought, compared to Mister Bilderbach's. Restlessness scattered her attention. She fumbled with her geometry book and "Le Voyage de Monsieur Perrichon" before putting them on the table. She sat down on the sofa and began to take her music from the satchel. Again she saw her hands—the quivering tendons that stretched down from her knuckles, the sore finger tip capped with curled, dingy tape. The sight sharpened the fear that had begun to torment her for the past few months.
>
> Noiselessly she mumbled a few phrases of encouragement to herself. A good lesson—a good lesson—like it used to be—Her lips closed as she heard the solid sound of Mister Bilderbach's footsteps across the floor of the studio and the creaking of the door as it slid open.

I'm afraid of Mr. Bilderbach myself, and he hasn't even stepped out to center stage yet. These characters are absolutely alive and real. The girl's fear is palpable. And why is this so? Because of the language. Look at these phrases.

> . . . her music satchel plopping against her winter-stock-
> inged legs and her other arm weighted down with school
> books . . .

This image leaps right off the page and into your mind. It isn't a complete description—short stories usually don't have room or time for head-to-toe descriptions—but it's enough. Besides, there's no reason to think that a description needs to be given all at once. It can be given piecemeal, the picture of the character gradually filling out in the first few pages of the story.

> Mister Bilderbach called out to her in his chunky, gut-
> tural tones.

"Guttural" is a common way to describe a voice, but combining it with "chunky" gives it a solidity that we will soon come to attribute to Bilderbach himself.

> As she jerked off her mittens she saw that her fingers
> were twitching to the motions of the fugue she had prac-
> ticed that morning.

How accurately this expresses her anxiety without the word "anxiety" or any of its synonyms being used.

> . . . his words spun out in a silky, unintelligible hum. A
> voice almost like a woman's. . .

Mr. Lafkowitz is drawn as an androgynous type chiefly by the words "spun" and "silky."

> . . . the quivering tendons that stretched down from her
> knuckles, the sore finger tip capped with curled, dingy tape.

Here we see that her pain is both physical and psychological. On the story's second page is the description of Bilderbach.

The quick eyes behind the horn-rimmed glasses; the light, thin hair and the narrow face beneath; the lips full and loose shut and the lower one pink and shining from the bites of his teeth; the forked veins in his temples throbbing plainly enough to be observed across the room.

Compare this to the following sentence.

"She was tall and willowy, and blessed with the natural dignity one usually associates with the aristocracy."

Of course there is no comparison. The first is etched with sharp detail. The second is pure abstract flab, powerless to evoke anything but a yawn.

Learn this lesson. Read McCullers' story. Pay close attention to the way she makes her characters real.

Here's what Joseph Conrad had to say on the subject: "My task is by power of the written word to make you hear, to make you feel—it is, before all, to make you see." Conrad was talking about all the processes that go into fiction writing, but it applies first and foremost to the establishment of character.

NOTICING THE DETAILS

Exercise

Here's an exercise in concentrated detail. People are spilling over with details. Go someplace where you can unobtrusively watch someone. A greasy-spoon cafe is as good a place as any. Bury yourself behind a newspaper. Don't read the newspaper. Turn all your attention to someone seated near enough to you so that you can see the lint on his or her coat. In your trusty notebook, make a list of ten or so noteworthy details about this person.

Example

black pants, too short.
brown topcoat. hole big as a quarter in lapel.

shoes held together with duct tape.
hair thick. matted with filth.
red bandanna around his neck.
head bowed, as if it were a painful weight.
large red hands, nails long and yellowing.
now and then chuckles soundlessly, as if secretly celebrating
    the genius of his thought processes.

Now put this character into a scene, drawing on the details you've recorded.

Example

> The old man from the park was in Safeway. He often hung around the parking lot, cadging spare change from shoppers pushing carts laden with groceries. He wore his usual uniform—black pants, brown topcoat buttoned all the way up. But tonight there was something new: he'd twisted a red bandanna around his skinny neck. The bandanna made a bold statement. It seemed to give him self-confidence. He smiled to himself, a wise smile, the smile of one who has solved one of life's basic problems. He didn't wander aimlessly through the aisles as usual, but went straight to the wine shelves. He slipped a pint of Mad Dog into his coat pocket, dropped another one on the floor. It exploded on the polished tiles. Then he walked without hurrying to the meat counter and stuffed his coat pockets with T-bones. He left the store, whistling, as the cleanup crews headed for the wine shelves with brooms, dustpans, and mops.

Do a bunch of these.

And make this part of your daily habit: Look at familiar people and things with such close attention that it seems you are seeing them for the first time. If you do this, you *will* be seeing them for the first time. You might be surprised by what you've missed. This habit is a requirement for painters. Bad painters give you no surprises—they give you expected landscapes, expected colors and shadings, expected faces. They may comfort but they never disturb or astonish or reveal. Good painters make you see how strangely unique each thing in the world is. A good painter can make an afternoon shadow falling across a carpet ominous, the ambiguity in a housewife's glance unsettling, the sky above a cemetery an ode to joy. One of my favorite paintings is Edward Hopper's study of a gas station just off a rural two-lane highway. The subject is ordinary, but his treatment of it is not. The painting never fails to give me the chills. What we do as fiction writers is not all that different from what painters do. We just paint our pictures with words.

We grow up accustomed to ignoring the details. We habitually move through the day with blinders on. This is probably necessary—if we let the full weight of the world press on our senses moment to moment, all day long, we'd be overwhelmed—but for someone who wants to see in the way an artist sees, this protective desensitizing is a real obstacle, a bad habit.

How do you break this habit? You have to work at it. Noticing the details takes conscious effort. We see only abbreviations of life because it takes time and effort to shed the blinders that prevent us from seeing it full-blown. We see people as blond, brunette, tall, short, thin, fat. We don't see how they fit in their clothes, the peculiarities of their movements, the expressions or lack of expressions on their faces, the way a hand gestures, the way an eye moves in its socket, how hair is made to obey or how it is in a condition of constant rebellion. We don't see the touch of grime on a coat sleeve, the long scratch on the back of a hand, the worn heel, the empty smile, the combative stiffening of a neck.

You need to see your characters with unsparing clarity if you expect a reader to see them at all.

Look how Raymond Chandler begins his long story "Trouble Is My Business."

> Anna Halsey was about two hundred and forty pounds
> of middle-aged putty-faced woman in a black tailor-made

suit. Her eyes were shiny black shoe buttons, her cheeks were as soft as suet and about the same color. She was sitting behind a black glass desk that looked like Napoleon's tomb and she was smoking a cigarette in a black holder that was not quite as long as a rolled umbrella. She said: "I need a man."

Regardless of what you might think of detective fiction and its conventions, Anna Halsey rises out of the page in three dimensions. She may be something of a caricature, but you can't *not* see her.

Skillful Description

Gustave Flaubert, speaking to his protégé Guy de Maupassant: "When you pass a grocer seated at his shop door, a janitor smoking his pipe, a stand of hackney coaches, show me that grocer and that janitor, their attitude, their whole physical appearance, including also by a skillful description their whole moral nature, so that I cannot confound them with any other grocer or any other janitor; make me see, in one word, that a certain cab horse does not resemble the fifty others that follow or precede it." And, ". . . there are not in the whole world two grains of sand, two specks, two hands, or two noses exactly alike. . . ."

With this excellent advice in mind, let's have another go at Sylvia and Lyle. Let's help the poor hack who's trying to become the human substitute for Sleep-Eze.

> Sylvia Merchant knocked on Lyle Nickerson's apartment door again, then tried the bell. She needed him to be in, hoped that he wasn't. If he was in, he was taking his time. He was probably standing at his bay window, watching traffic. Humiliation for Lyle was an art form.
>
> Sylvia had failed, she knew that. She'd made a stupid choice, and was ashamed and angry about it. She'd paid for twelve "consultations" but had endured only six. Even so she was not willing to cut her losses. She wanted her

money back. Every wasted dollar. The man was a fraud, a human lamprey. The door opened a crack.

"It's not Wednesday," Lyle said through the still-chained door. Sylvia could see his full lips, fringed with silky black hair, his slender nose with its pinched nostrils.

"It's Wednesday," Sylvia said. She felt confident, and she knew she looked good: pink silk tunic and black skirt, black slingback sandals, her makeup understated, her nails glossy black. Intimidating black.

"Wednesday, really?" Lyle said. "Is that you, Sylvia?"

The chain dropped against the jamb and the door swung open. Lyle was wearing his maroon smoking jacket with the shiny satin lapels, dark blue slacks, and patent leather slip-ons. He was thin but gave the impression of largeness. His small pot belly pushed against the sash of his jacket. He was only forty, yet his long neck was loose with the beginnings of a wattle. He fished a cigarette out of a crumpled pack. He used a cigarette holder, his fingers nicotine-stained from years of smoking without one. When he looked at her, his stare was direct and cool as if assessing her and she realized that this was only a technique, something he no doubt used on all the women who came to him. Before becoming a self-styled writing teacher in Slocum Falls, Indiana, he'd been the society editor for a Palm Beach weekly. "A While With Lyle," a tenth-page, Section D feature.

"*Entrez, cheri*," he said.

Sylvia stepped into the apartment. Every time she came here she felt she was entering a movie set. The interior was straight out of 1930, uncompromised art deco. There was no TV set of course, but there was a perfect replica of a console radio made entirely of white Bakelite. It sat against a wall between a pair of overstuffed Jean-Michel Frank love seats—love seats that looked both sumptuous and severe. The oyster white walls held framed posters of Josephine Baker's *La Revue Nègre*. Sylvia imagined the bathroom: all glass and black tile, oversized chrome faucets and taps, an ostentatious bidet. Lyle's concert grand dominated the living room. The piano was the focus of the apartment, the gravitational center that commanded attention. Next to it, an ebony Brancusi head stared sightlessly from a fluted pedestal.

Sylvia found the apartment both ludicrous and oppressive. She almost felt sorry for the man who lived here. She understood that Lyle was just another phony, a bitter man whose own mediocrity had exiled him to Slocum Falls where he'd played the big fish in a small pond. He'd impressed a lot of people since he'd arrived. Sylvia included. She couldn't believe that she'd been infatuated with him.

"I'm quitting," she said.

"*Quitting?*" Lyle said. A thin smile raised the corners of his lips but his heavy-lidded eyes were dull with disinterest. "Quitting what you haven't started? *Quelle dommage.* I thought better of you. You seemed . . . more serious than the others. The matrons of Slocum Falls! They've confused their boredom with the urge to create! They can't settle for what they are: talentless wanna-bes hoping to be thought of as one of this jerkwater town's artistic types. They've never lived but they want to write about *life*! Why don't they simply join a reading club—and be done with it?" He punctuated his lecture with quick sips from his cigarette holder. His voice was darkly musical, seductive as a cello. "I should not have allowed you to continue past the first lesson—mea culpa, my dear."

"I want my three hundred dollars," Sylvia said, unable to keep the waver out of her voice.

Lyle took her hand in his. It appalled her that the soft pressure of his grip was comforting, that his voice still had the weight of authority. She bit her lip; she had no confidence at all. She was a Slocum Falls girl, born and raised. A cheerleader for Slocum Falls High, the receptionist for

The Slocum Falls Clinic, and daughter of Slocum Falls' only chiropodist.

"Don't cry, Sylvia," Lyle said. "Look, I'm damned sorry. I've had a hellishly rotten day. Erase what I said. I didn't mean it. You're not like them. You *do* have ability, really. The talent is there—you just need discipline. Let me take you to dinner—we'll talk about it."

Will she or won't she? We'll never know. The story, if there is one, is probably not worth telling simply because it's stale and predictable. But the point is that these characters, familiar as they are, can now be *seen* and *heard*. Even their moral nature has been touched upon. The writer now can even get away with a little abstractifying: The sofa looks "both sumptuous and severe." Once you've set the scene in concrete, you can afford to dress up an object with invisible qualities, and, in this case, these invisible qualities provide another, more oblique, way to assess Lyle's character.

Listen to what Wilkie Collins had to say, over a hundred years ago: "It may be possible to present character successfully without telling a story; but it is not possible to tell a story without presenting characters: their existence, as recognisable realities, being the sole condition on which the story can be effectively told. The only narrative which can hope to lay a strong hold on the attention of readers is a narrative which interests them about men and women—for the perfectly obvious reason that they are men and women themselves."

If there are any absolutes in short story writing, this comes as close as any to being one.

MOTIVATION: THE ENGINE OF "WANT"

Fiction is about trouble. Trouble is a direct consequence of desire. Characters are living embodiments of desire. A character without desire is immobilized. A corpse is without desire.

We grow up into a world of desire. All of us do—there are no exceptions. The extinction of desire is the goal of Buddhist philosophy. It isn't easy. It takes total commitment, a lifetime of discipline. Few succeed.

But writers don't create characters who have been enlightened beyond all desire. Contemporary fiction is about people who want something and don't know how to get it or are prevented—by internal or external forces—from finding it. Or if they get what they want, it's not what it seemed when it only existed as a desire. (One of my characters in a moment of insight says, "Better to be sustained in exile by a dream of home rather than to endure the disappointments of home itself.") The commercial fiction of fifty years ago was about characters achieving—after the necessary setbacks and delays—the objects of their desires. This type of fiction has been appropriated by the movies.

The object of a character's desire could be a common thing, such as a job, a companion, an inheritance. Or it could be a less well-defined thing, such as the expiation of guilt, emotional survival, a second chance, freedom from baseless fear, the hope that another might change his or her unacceptable behavior. And so on. *A character in need is the force that sets a story in motion.*

Sometimes the desire that motivates a character is not obvious for this reason: Many people don't know what they want; they just *want*. There's an empty place in the core of their being that requires occupancy. But what can fill it? Want itself can't—want is only the engine of acquisition. But the relentless pressure of wanting motivates them to act out, in some way, desires that have become abstract. Such characters need to solve the undefined mystery central to their lives, but, because they can't define it, they function in a fog of confusion and doubt. They may seem sure-footed, and their lives may appear to have a positive direction, but they are in a bog, sinking.

The beginning of Elio Vittorini's short novel *In Sicily* starts out, "That winter I was haunted by abstract furies." Abstract furies resist definition. Vittorini's character feels emotionally dead, but is moved nonetheless by some subterranean impulse to revisit his hometown in Sicily, where the main action of the story takes place. His abstract desires lead him to a series of interviews with the people he knew when he was a child. But all the conversations he has with them are, somehow, off the point. They seem like coded exchanges, coded because the abstract furies that haunt him can't be addressed directly. *In Sicily* is the story of a soul fighting to restore the life that has been bled out of it. It's an odd book—wandering and plotless—but compelling nonetheless because we believe in the seriousness of the central character's need.

The Character's Needs

The actions of characters, whether misguided, random, well-planned, cowardly, or heroic, depend on how close their individual quests are to their actual needs. As readers we hope, by story's end, that we have some idea of what's been troubling them. Sometimes we won't, and one reader's guess is as good as another's. But in any case, we need to believe that what they *do* has a genuine motive.

A character who wants something he or she can't define can become vulnerable to whatever comes along that seems to fill the need. Sherwood Anderson might well be the godfather of this kind of story. Much of contemporary fiction is about such characters. They populate the work of Alice Munro and Joyce Carol Oates and countless others. In Flannery O'Connor's story "Good Country People," the focus of the story is Hulga, a thirty-two-year-old virgin who has a Ph.D. in philosophy. Hulga thinks she has arrived at a terminal understanding of life ("I don't have illusions. I am one of those people who sees *through* to nothing," she boasts) and requires little else. But her undefined needs are brought to the surface by the devious Bible salesman who seduces her and then steals her artificial leg. Her sophistication is academic only. Hulga doesn't know herself, but the uneducated Bible salesman knows perfectly well who *he* is.

Self-knowledge comes with a price. In Raymond Carver's "The Compartment," the principal character, Myers, thinks he wants a reconciliation with his estranged son. Myers's marriage has broken up, the son had been difficult to raise, and Myers is guilt-ridden but also full of undefined rage. The son is in France, attending the university in Strasbourg. Myers, responding to a letter from his son, flies to Europe. On the train to Strasbourg, Myers has a realization.

> It came to him that he didn't want to see the boy after all. He was shocked by this realization and for a moment felt diminished by the meanness of it. He shook his head. In a lifetime of foolish actions, this trip was possibly the most foolish thing he'd ever done. But the fact was, he really had no desire to see this boy whose behavior had long ago isolated him from Myers's affections.

We like to think of ourselves as noble, or if not noble, at least decent and responsible. We always try to do our best, don't we? Writers like Raymond Carver have the ability to pry into the cracks of personality, exposing the feelings and impulses that contradict a character's cherished self-image.

> The boy had devoured Myers's youth, had turned the young girl he had courted and wed into a nervous, alcoholic woman whom the boy alternately pitied and bullied. Why on earth, Myers asked himself, would he come all this way to see someone he disliked?

This is a stunning revelation, perhaps too difficult for most people in similar circumstances to accept. But Myers accepts it; he doesn't get off the train at Strasbourg. He's confronted his moral dilemma: paternal duty versus his true feelings. His ultimate decision can be seen as a moral failure, but it can also be seen as honest self-acceptance. Myers will not lie about his feelings—either to his son or to himself. The reconciliation is postponed, perhaps abandoned beyond rescue.

In Tobias Wolff's story "Face to Face," a lonely woman is matched by a friend with a man who is equally alone and lonely. Both characters, Virginia and Robert, want someone to love. They are motivated. But while Virginia is honest with herself, and with Robert, Robert is emotionally evasive. Robert seems to want a companion, someone to share his life with, but he is awkward and shy and treats sex as if it's some tedious requirement to get out of the way as quickly and as impersonally as possible. He is not capable of intimacy. In truth, Robert doesn't want Virginia or anyone else. He's destined to be a loner. When she tells him, after a strained moment, that it's natural for lonely people to look for someone to love, Robert looks "at her with sudden panic and she knew that he was deciding at that moment always to be alone."

Motives

Why we do what we do is a main concern of the contemporary fiction writer. I suppose it has been a main concern of the literary arts since the ancient Greeks. The Greeks had answers—the gods compel, favor, and punish—but all we have are the insights of our best artists. Some writers, such as Flannery O'Connor, infuse religious faith into their work. In O'Connor's stories, the Christian notions of grace and redemption have deterministic functions. O'Connor, however, insists that her "beliefs are not what I see but the light by which I see." In other words, she doesn't offer easy, prepackaged solutions—an aesthetically disastrous thing for any writer to do—but allows her characters the freedom to be themselves, regardless of the outcome, in a world that O'Connor sees as fallen from grace.

Your job, as a writer of short fiction—whatever your beliefs— is to put complex personalities on stage and let them strut and fret their brief hour. Perhaps the sound and fury they make will signify something that has more than passing value—that will, in Chekhov's words, "make [man] see what he is like."

I have sometimes written a dozen or more pages and have not been able to grasp what my character was all about. The writing— for whatever reason—might have been engaging, but because I could not figure out what was motivating my character, the accumulating pages added up to nothing. I didn't know whom I was dealing with. I didn't know what he or she wanted.

If *motive* is missing, your character can go through all sorts of delightful or hair-raising adventures and it won't add up to a hill of beans. A character who is merely interesting is never enough. I see interesting characters every day, have met them all my life. So have you. But without the engine of "want" pulling at them, they will never give you a story.

Exercise

Think of a character who wants something badly. This should be easy. You've wanted something badly at one point or another in your life. It could be an abstract thing, such as the respect of an employer, self-respect, reciprocated love, the loyalty of a spouse, the appreciation of a parent, and so on. Or it could be something tangible—money; a prized antique; a new well that produces clean, clear water; great-grandfather's 1928 touring car that's still in pristine condition. The need could also be for a combination of the abstract and the tangible—the physical object and the abstract longing becoming identified with each other in the character's mind. For example, a man who has found little satisfaction as a Wall Street stockbroker sees the acquisition of a ranch in Colorado as the key to regaining his self-respect.

You get the idea. Now, put your character in a setting in which the thing he or she wants is being denied by circumstances or by another person. Write a page or two in which the need of the character is serious enough to suggest that a strong story follows.

Example

Doug Crawford was the New Jersey salesman for the Triple A Folding Box Company, but his heart was never in it. Doug's heart belonged to golf. He had won the club championship at Twelve Oaks seven times, the county championship four and the state twice. Three times he had qualified for the National Open. Every fall when the northern courses began to freeze and the birds and the pros headed south he would try to decide between staying with [his job] and playing professionally on the winter tour. Every year for the past eight he'd come up with the same decision. His game wasn't quite ready; he would stay with Triple A one more year.

—From "200,000 Dozen Pairs of Socks"
by William Price Fox

This sets the stage for what follows. It's a fine story, a heartbreaker about a dream denied.

6

PLOT VS. STORY

A story without a plot is like a house with no hallways or rooms, just nooks and crannies. Which is fine. I like open space; I like nooks and crannies. Most contemporary short stories are thin on plot. They have a lot of space and light in them, and the surprises are in the subtleties of detail, mood, and behavior, not in the architecture.

John Cheever had little use for plots. In a *Paris Review* interview, he said, "I don't work with plots. I work with intuition, apprehension, dreams, concepts. Characters and events come simultaneously to me. [Plot] is an attempt to hold the reader's interest at the sacrifice of moral conviction. Of course, one doesn't want to be boring . . . one needs an element of suspense. But a good narrative is a rudimentary structure, rather like a kidney."

And yet it sometimes seems a good idea to begin in mystery so that you can end in revelation. Somerset Maugham put it succinctly: "The author always loads his dice, but he must never let the reader see that he has done so, and by the manipulation of his plot, he can engage the reader's attention so that he does not perceive what violence has been done to him."

EVENTS AND ANTECEDENT EVENTS

Here's an example of plotless writing:

I drove to town. It was a hot afternoon. In J.C. Penney's

I bought a short-sleeve shirt. Then I had a light lunch. After that I went to Wilma's apartment. She wasn't in. I waited on the front steps of the building. The late afternoon sun sent broad shafts of yellow light between the elms that lined her street. I lit a cigarette.

Here's the same basic story structure complicated by plot.

I decided to drive into town after all. My first stop was J.C. Penney's, where I bought the kind of shirt I used to wear when I was riding high—golf logos on the pockets. I left my old sweat-sopped shirt in a trash basket in the dressing room. It looked like someone had died miserably in it. It made me smile. In the full-length mirror my smile looked more like a rictus snarl. I paid the clerk with my last fifty and headed for the nearest McDonald's, where I ordered three quarter-pounders and black coffee. Then I went to Wilma's place, knowing what a damned fool I was for thinking she'd welcome me with open arms, but she wasn't in. Why did I think she'd wait for me? No matter. I waited for her, on her front steps. I'd been waiting for ten years. Another hour or two would be easy. Even in this heat and killer sun.

In the first paragraph, the events described are purely sequential and are untainted by history: They have no antecedent events to give them significance. The only question the reader will ask—if the writing is interesting enough—is, What happens next?

In the second paragraph, every gesture or observation is rooted in some prior event of real significance to the narrator. The reader asks not only what happens next but what happened to this man *before* this initial paragraph.

At this point in the story, the antecedent events are unknown to the reader. Some or all may be revealed eventually, thus providing the story with causative factors. (Metafictionists have played with this idea by inventing situations that are connected to antecedents, but the antecedents are never revealed, keeping the mystery hermetically sealed.)

The aggregate of hidden, causative factors makes up the *plot*. Plot is the story behind the story. This is obviously the case in detective fiction. There can be no mystery without the hidden "true" story lurking behind the tangle of false leads. The detective—the reader's surrogate—is the truth seeker.

Admittedly, the second paragraph is heavily laced with dramatic bait. It isn't necessary to be so heavy-handed. What makes this paragraph heavy-handed is the number of significant events that lie behind it: "I decided to drive into town after all." (Our narrator has been weighing the decision to go into town. Why? Is he a wanted criminal? Does he need to avoid someone he might meet in town? Is he agoraphobic? Or is he just bored with the town itself?) "My first stop was J.C. Penney's, where I bought the kind of shirt I used to wear when I was riding high. . . ." (He once was up, but now he's down. Why is that?) "I left my old sweat-sopped shirt in a trash basket in the dressing room. It looked like someone had died miserably in it. It made me smile." (Has he been roughed up? Has he been living for months in boxcars and hobo jungles? And what's so funny about it?) "In the full-length mirror my smile looked more like a rictus snarl." (So it's not funny. But why this dissociation between his emotions and his facial expression? What awful things have happened to him that he snarls when he thinks he's smiling?) "Then I went to Wilma's place, knowing what a damned fool I was for thinking she'd welcome me with open arms. . . ." (Ending the paragraph this way lets the reader know the story will unfold in a way that will be more or less determined by the history of the narrator's relationship with Wilma, the major antecedent event of the story.)

The second paragraph illustrates the point, but you wouldn't want to open a story this way. There's too much violence being done to pique the reader's curiosity. The drumbeat is too heavy; it drowns out the subtler instruments.

Let's see how some famous stories suggest antecedent events

more subtly, thus creating plot. Here is the opening paragraph of Katherine Anne Porter's "Flowering Judas":

> Braggioni sits heaped upon the edge of a straight-backed chair much too small for him, and sings to Laura in a furry, mournful voice. Laura has begun to find reasons for avoiding her own house until the latest possible moment, for Braggioni is there almost every night. No matter how late she is, he will be sitting there with a surly, waiting expression, pulling at his kinky yellow hair, thumbing the strings of his guitar, snarling a tune under his breath. Lupe the Indian maid meets Laura at the door, and says with a flicker of a glance towards the upper room, "He waits."

Clearly the story is being propelled by antecedent events. This Braggioni character is Laura's (apparently necessary) burden, has been for some time, and she evidently cannot find a way to be free of him. All this raises questions in the mind of the reader, questions that compel the reader to read on.

Here is the brief opening paragraph of Henry James' "Paste":

> "I've found a lot more things," her cousin said to her the day after the second funeral; "they're up in her room—but they're things I wish *you'd* look at."

Here we have a trio of antecedent events: the second funeral—whose was the first?—and the things found in the deceased's room, things with a history of special interest to the principal character.

And this is from the opening paragraph of John Cheever's "The Five Forty-Eight":

> When Blake stepped out of the elevator, he saw her. A few people, mostly men waiting for girls, stood in the lobby watching the elevator doors. She was among them. As he saw her, her face took on a look of such loathing and purpose that he realized she had been waiting for him. . . . He turned and walked toward the glass doors at the end of the

lobby, feeling that faint guilt and bewilderment we experience when we bypass some old friend or classmate who seems threadbare, or sick, or miserable in some other way. . . . Outside, he started walking briskly east toward Madison Avenue. . . . The sidewalk was crowded. He wondered what she had hoped to gain by a glimpse of him coming out of the office building at the end of the day. Then he wondered if she was following him.

This paragraph is loaded but not overloaded. We need to know what the woman's motives are and what's going to happen to Blake. If you've read this much of Cheever's story, you're going to want to read more.

THE IMPLIED ANTECEDENT EVENT

All the above paragraphs—all by writers who have had a major influence on the contemporary short story—have this in common: Something of consequence has happened; something of further consequence is about to happen.

But not all short stories begin with such dramatic couplings between what has happened and what is bound to happen. Some begin in an objective presentation of a scene, as in Ernest Hemingway's "Hills Like White Elephants." The antecedent event(s) in this story have to be culled from the dialogue between its two characters, the man and the woman waiting for the express train from Barcelona. The dialogue is neutral at first. Then tension is introduced.

The girl was looking off at the line of hills. They were white in the sun and the country was brown and dry.

"They look like white elephants," she said.

"I've never seen one," the man drank his beer.

"No, you wouldn't have."

"I might have," the man said. "Just because you say I wouldn't have doesn't prove anything."

The girl's tone is accusatory; his is defensive. And now, since there has been no hint of a conflict up to this point, either in the dialogue or the imagery, and the atmosphere is neutral, we have to wonder what's gone wrong, what's happened between them. This then is the first implication of plot. But it's only a tease. Hemingway backs off, allows the dialogue to become relaxed again. It's not until fourteen lines of dialogue later that the tension is reintroduced after they've ordered *anis*.

> "It tastes like licorice," the girl said and put the glass down.
>
> "That's the way with everything."
>
> "Yes," said the girl. "Everything tastes of licorice. Especially all the things you've waited so long for, like absinthe."
>
> "Oh, cut it out."
>
> "You started it," the girl said. "I was being amused. I was having a fine time."
>
> "Well, let's try to have a fine time."

This game (petulant enough to make us realize these are very young people) goes on, the intensity gradually building. The mystery becomes clear: She's become pregnant and he wants her to have an abortion; she wants the child, and perhaps a stable life. This is the dramatic core of the plot. The story is (as in all the above examples) greater than the plot. "Hills Like White Elephants" is about that point in life where one either accepts the responsibility for one's actions or continues to live selfishly, as though those actions had no consequence of any importance. The plot in this story instigates mystery and provides tension. It is vital to the structure of the story (and thus to its effect), but it is an architectural schematic only, a way to secure its impact.

THE OPEN-ENDED STORY

If plot has a bad name among contemporary short story writers, I think it's because of a trend in the form established early in the twentieth century by writers such as O. Henry, Saki (H.H. Munro), and their many imitators who wrote very entertaining stories in which plot was everything, when it wasn't the story behind the story but the story itself. They were masters of a certain kind of story, but the effect depended on the writer's ability to manipulate the reader. "Clever" is the adjective you think of when you think of these writers. It is difficult to read one of their surprise-ending stories twice, since the main effect is the surprise itself. Once the surprise is known, the story—like a joke heard more than once—loses its ability to entertain.

I don't mean to offend fans of these writers—I still enjoy them myself from time to time. Saki's "The Open Window" is a gem. Cleverness sometimes is enough. But the rhetoric of these stories is typically arch, as if the author were encouraging the reader, from the outset, to participate in the joke. You can almost sense the author winking at the reader. This technique gradually came into disfavor, especially when a new breed of short story writers began to dominate the form with works that staked out richer—and more serious—territory.

Chekhov, Joyce, Sherwood Anderson, among others less well known, created a new trend: the open-ended story, the story in which plot is almost nonexistent and character is everything.

By open-ended I mean that the "resolution" of the story is not dramatically conclusive. The reader is left with an impression of life rather than with the "satisfying" conclusion a heavily plotted story must deliver. And yet the open-ended story must also leave the reader satisfied. But here the satisfaction comes from an understanding that all that can be said *has* been said. The reader should not require more than what has been given.

For example: Suppose you're writing a story in which the concluding scene has a man and a woman canoeing on a river. Suppose, like the Hemingway story, something has gone wrong with their relationship. Suppose further that the couple haven't been paying attention to where they've drifted or how long they've been out on the river and that they are inexperienced with canoes in general and with rivers in particular. And now night is coming on and the wind is cold. Suddenly they find themselves shivering in the dark. The increasing sound of rapids can be heard. In an open-ended story, there should be no need to carry them into the perilous rapids. The story is what happened between the two that led to this dangerous moment. The story could end this way.

> He heard the roar of water descending over large stones. The river's voice, which for the last two hours had been a whisper, now rose like ten thousand shouting soldiers anticipating the enemy.

Dramatic maybe, but not dramatically *conclusive* at all—we'll never know what happened to the couple. But if the writer has made it clear that everything we need to know about them has been given earlier, we won't now require a life-and-death struggle in the rapids. In fact, that might be anticlimactic and lead the story (as well as the writer) into inextricable confusion.

In 1926 Thomas Hardy, complaining to Virginia Woolf about a work of Aldous Huxley's, said, "They've changed everything now. . . . We used to think there was a beginning and a middle and an end. We believed in the Aristotelian theory. Now one of those stories came to an end with a woman going out of a room."

Here is an open-ended story of mine that tried awfully hard to be closed-ended. I wrote it early in my writing career (though it's undergone several rewrites since then) when I was still unsure of how to bring a story to a satisfactory close.

THE SMILE OF A TURTLE

> Cobb knows the cooped housewives need him. A new breed of degenerate (de-gents, Cobb calls them) has been making the headlines. A door-to-door salesman with a sharp yen for the average, haggard, wide-beam housewife. Cobb saw it in the *Times* yesterday morning. This de-gent peddling a glass knife guaranteed to slice overripe tomatoes. College educated guy at that. Nice, trim, clean-cut, good suit from Bullock's or Macy's, and this normally

cautious housewife *lets him in*. He demonstrated his glass knife on her. Sliced her, diced her, iced her. Then went out to his Volvo to jerk off. Bad news. The bad old world is full of it, but Cobb's product promises freedom from such bad dreams. He holds the three-inch chrome-plated cylinder up to the cracked (but still chained) door so that the lady can see it clearly. His blond, unlined face looks harmless and sincere and deeply concerned about Home Security. It's his business, and Cobb has been working the hot neighborhoods of West L.A. all morning this burning day in early August.

"You need this device, ma'am," Cobb says, sincere as the Eagle Scout he once was. "Every housewife in L.A. needs it. A simple demonstration will make this abundantly clear. The de-gents, ma'am, are everywhere." He says "ma'am" in the soft southern way to slow her trotting heart. But the gadget sells itself. And it's a bargain at five dollars. Ten would be fair and most would pay twenty, but all he wants is the price of a movie ticket. Isn't home security worth at least that much—the price, say, of *Friday the 13th Part Three* or *Dressed to Kill*?

She opens the door a hair wider, hooked. Cobb looks like her kid brother, or her old high school boyfriend, or maybe the nice boy who delivers the paper. All American Cleancut. He looks harmless as a puppy. There's even something cuddly about him, something you could pet. A dancing prickle of heat glides across the nape of her neck and into her hair line.

Cobb is working on projecting these positive vibes. He feels that he's able, now, to radiate serious alpha waves. His boss, Jake the Distributor, has this theory. He thinks every man and woman is an animal at heart. We respond, he says, to the animal in each other. We see it in our little unconscious moves and gestures. We see it in our eyes. The trick, says Jake the Distributor, is to identify *your* personal animal and let the pure alpha waves flow out of it. This is how you become a world-class salesman. Jake the Distributor has studied the subject in depth. "You," he said to Cobb, "are obviously a turtle." He said this at a big sales meeting and everyone laughed. Turtle, what good is a turtle, Cobb thought, humiliated, and, as if answering his thoughts, someone hollered, "Soup! Soup!" and they all laughed at him and among the laughers he identified the barking hyenas and dogs, the hooting chimps and gibbons, and the softly hissing turtles.

Cobb bought Jake the Distributor's theory. He made a study of turtles. The Chinese had some definite ideas about them, for instance. On the plus side, turtles are careful and shy, fond of warm mud, and ready to leave a bad scene at the first sign of trouble. On the minus side, they are shifty, shiftless, and dirty-minded. They think about getting it morning, noon, and night. They are built for getting it. Even their tails help out. The turtle tail is prehensile during the act. It holds the female close and tight and there's no way she can detach herself once things get under way. Turtles can screw ten, fifteen times a day and not lose interest.

But Jake the Distributor says, Emphasize the positive and you will make your fortune. Keep your fingernails clean and clipped. Wash up several times a day—you can develop a bad stink walking the neighborhoods all day long. Change your shorts. Use a strong underarm spray. Don't touch yourself out of habit in the area of your privates while in the process of making a pitch. Keep a good shine on your shoes. Keep your nap up. Hair trimmed and combed. Teeth white, breath sweet, pits dry. Groom, groom, groom.

It's the brace-and-bit, though, that tends to do major harm to his first good impression. This can't be helped—tools of the trade. Cobb tries to hold it down behind his leg. But she's seen it and is holding her breath. So he starts his pitch, talking fast. "It's called Cyclops, ma'am," he says. (Southern, says Jake the Distributor, don't forget to sound southern. They *trust* southern. Sound New York and you are dead meat in the street. Sound L.A. and you get no pay. Think genteel, southern Mississippi. Think graceful Georgia. But do not think Okie. Talk Okie and they will pee their drawers. Bike gangs are Okie. Bible salesmen are weirdo Okie. Think magnolia blossoms and buggy whips and mint juleps. Think *Gone With the Wind.* Make them think they are Scarlet O'Hara.) "The *Farrago* Cyclops, ma'am," Cobb explains. "Charles V. Farrago being the name of the gentleman who invented it and who currently holds the exclusive manufacturing rights. Yes, there are many cheap imitations, ma'am, but there is only one Farrago Cyclops!"

She stands there blinking in the crack of the chained door. She's a *mouse*, Cobb begins to realize. Thirty-five to forty, afraid of sudden moves and noise, bright outdoor light always a threat, for there are hawks, there are cats. Her house is dark inside, like a nest chewed into wood by quick, small teeth. She is wearing a gray housecoat and she is nibbling something—a piece of cheese!—and Cobb almost grins in her face, pleased that he's identified her secret animal so perfectly.

He fights back his knowing smile, for the smile of a turtle is a philosophical thing. It tends to put things into long-term perspective. It makes the recipient think: there's more to this situation than I presently understand. It will give the recipient a chill. A mouse will run from such a smile, though in nature mice and turtles are not enemies. But, Cobb thinks, we are not in nature. This is L.A., this is the world. He masters the smile and muscles it back to where it came from.

"Here you go, ma'am," he says. "Take it. Try it." She receives it gingerly, as if it were a loaded gun with a hair trigger. *Microtus pennsylvanicus*, Cobb thinks, mouse, and that is what she surely was meant to be, down to the cream cheese marrow of her small bones. He begins to think of her as "Minnie."

Cobb kneels down suddenly on her welcome mat. Stitched into the sisal mat are the letters of a Spanish word, *bienvenido*. He crouches down as low as he can get. Neighborhood children freeze with curiosity on their skateboards. The heat leans down through the perpetually grainy sky. In the north, the annual arsonists have set fire to the brushy hills. In the east, flash floods. Rapists, stranglers, and slashers roam the jammed tract-house valleys. Santa Ana wind, moaning in the TV antennas, spills over the mountains from the desert, electrifying the air. The ionized air lays a charge on the surface of his skin, the hair of his arms stands up stiff and surly, as if muscled, and his brain feels tacked into its casing. His back is soaked with sweat and his pits are swamps.

"Sometimes these de-gents will ring your bell, ma'am," he says, "and then drop down to all fours like this hoping that the lady occupant, such as yourself, will make the fatal mistake of opening the door to see what's going on even though she didn't see anybody in the peephole. Some of these de-gents are real weasels, take my word for it. But the Farrago Cyclops will expose them, due to the fish-eye lens system." And he can see now that she is suddenly gripped by the idea of the sort of weasel who would ring her bell and then hide on her doorstep, waiting to spring.

"The worst is sure to happen, ma'am," he says, gravely, "sooner or later, because of the nature of the perverted mind in today's world. This is a proven statistical fact, known to most as Murphy's Law." Cobb makes a movement with his wrist, suggesting a weapon. Sledge, ax, awl, ice pick, the rapist's long razor, the slasher's stiletto. He shows her some crotch bulge, the possible avenger in there, coiled to strike. "You *can* see me, ma'am?" he asks. She gives one nod, her face crimped up as she peers into the Cyclops. "That's it, ma'am," says Cobb, doing Georgia, doing 'Bama. "Hold it level to the ground, as if it was already in place in your door."

"You look sort of funny," she says. "Oblong. Or top-heavy."

"It's the lens, ma'am. Fish-eye. It puts a bend in the world, but you get to see more of it that way."

Cobb stands up and makes a quick pencil mark on the door. "Right about here, I guess. What are you, ma'am, about five foot one?" She nods. "Husband gone most of the day? His work take him out of town a lot? You spend a lot of time alone?" She looks like a fading photograph of herself. Cobb stops his grin before it crawls into his lips. He raises the brace-and-bit, pauses just long enough to get her consent, which she gives by stepping backward a few inches and turning her head slightly to one side, a gesture of acquiescence, and Cobb scores the flimsy laminated wood with the tip of the bit and starts the hole, one inch in diameter, right on the pencil mark, level with her wide open eyes. He leans on the brace and cranks. The wood is tract-house cheap, false grain, oak, hollow, so thin a child could kick a hole in it.

To see how fast her door can be penetrated unsettles her and so Cobb tries to calm her down with a brief outline of the Charles V. Farrago success story. Rags to riches in the Home Security field. From shop mechanic to multimillionaire. From Cedar Rapids to Carmel by the Sea. The undisputed king of home surveillance devices. A genius by any standard. Cobb carries a photograph of Charles V. Farrago and promises to show it to the woman as soon as he drills out her door. In the photograph, taken some twenty or thirty years ago, Farrago has a big round head and a smile that goes two hands across with more teeth in it than seem possible. He has shrewd little eyes that preside above the smile like twin watchdogs.

Cobb tells the woman other stories. He tells her about the woman, housewife like herself, who had oil of vitriol pumped up her nose through one of those old fashioned door-peepers. Knock knock, and she opened the little peeper to see who was there and it was a de-gent. Splat. Blinded for life and horribly disfigured all for the want of a proper doorstep surveillance device. Blue crater where once was her nose, upper lip a leather flap, eyes milky clouds. The reason? No *reason*. There never is a reason. It was a prank. The de-gent chemistry student had seen *Phantom of the Opera* on TV. It was Halloween in Denver or Salt Lake or Omaha. A few years ago. He told the police: "I just had this big urge to melt a face, you know?"

Cobb tells her the one about the naked de-gent who knocked on a peeperless door and said, "Parcel Post!" He made love to his victim with a gardening tool right in front of her little kids. He left a red hoofprint on her shag carpet and that's how the cops caught him: his right foot had only two toes and the print looked cloven, like it had been left by a goat. The *Times* called him "The Goatfoot Gasher."

The grumbling bit chews through the last laminations of veneer and Cobb reaches around the still-chained door to catch the curls of blond wood which he puts into his shirt pocket. Do not leave an unsightly mess, says Jake the Distributor. Be neat as a pin. Cobb inserts the Cyclops gently and with a little sigh into the tight hole then screws on the locking flange. "Let's give it a try, ma'am," he says.

She closes the door and Cobb goes out to the sidewalk. He stands still long enough for her to get used to the odd shapes the fish-eye lens produces, then starts to move down the sidewalk in big sidesteps to the other extreme of her vision. He approaches the house on the oblique, crossing the lawn, dropping behind a shrub, reemerging on hands and knees, moving swiftly now like a Dirty Dozen commando toward the welcome mat. He knows what she is seeing, knows how the lens makes him look heavy through the middle, pin-headed, legs stubby, his shined shoes fat as seals, the mean unsmiling lips, the stumpy bulge at the apex of his fat thighs, the neighborhood curving around him like a psychopathic smirk.

"It really *works*," she says, showing as much enthusiasm as she feels she can afford when Cobb reappears at the door, brushing off his knees and smiling like a helpful Scout. She slips a five dollar bill through the cracked door and Cobb notices that it has been folded into a perfect square the size of a stamp.

"Satisfaction fully guaranteed, ma'am," he says, unfolding, meticulously, the bill. A fragrance, trapped in the bill for possibly years, makes his nostrils flare.

Cobb winks and the woman allows herself a coo of gratitude. Turtle and mouse rapport, Cobb thinks, pleased. This is what you strive for, says Jake the Distributor. Cross the species lines. This is the hallmark of the true salesman. Make them think you are just like them, practically *kin*, though we know that this is basically laughable.

This is Cobb's tenth sale this morning. He keeps one dollar and fifteen cents out of every five. On good days he'll sell fifty. But today won't be a good day—for sales, at least. Too hot. He feels as if there's this big unfair hand in the sky that's been lowering all morning, pushing him down. He needs a break. He needs to cool off, wash up—a nice shower would do it—he needs to get out of his swampy shirt, air his pits and the steaming crotch of his slacks. He wants to use her john, but he knows her mouse heart will panic if he asks. Instead, he asks if he can use her phone. "Need to check in," he explains, his voice decent, a fellow human being making a reasonable request, a finely honed act. She fades a bit, but she is not a swift thinker and can't find a way to say no pleasantly. Cobb has his Eagle Scout glow turned up full blast. His boylike vulnerability is apparent in the bend of his spine, put there by the unfair bone-warping hand that presses down on him from the dirty sky, trying to make him crawl again, but he is through crawling today and is ready to lay claim to the small things of this world that should be his, but are not. The woman slides the chained bolt out of its slot and opens the door wide in jerky, indecisive increments.

"Oh, lady," he says, his voice relaxing now into its natural cadence. "You're the angel of mercy in the flesh. Really." Cobb, hard thin lips flexed in a triumphant V, walks in.

In the first few drafts of this story, I had Cobb entering the woman's house, using her bathroom, using her telephone, making himself generally at home while becoming more and more threatening. I couldn't bring myself to follow the logic all the way through and have Cobb rape and/or kill her. Something in me (let's call it good taste) balked at this. Had I allowed Cobb to complete the course of action he was apparently set on, the story would have been meaningless. How could I answer the question—a question every writer has to ask at some point during the composition of a story—What is my story about? If Cobb had raped and/or murdered the woman, my story would have been about this: A door-to-door salesman of dubious stability rapes and/or murders a housewife. This is not a short story; this is a news item.

I was stuck with Cobb hanging around, making a nuisance of himself, and in the process wrecking my story by turning it into a sinister farce. Around the fifth or sixth rewrite, the idea occurred to me to end the thing just as the woman opens the door for him— a much more chilling ending than anything I could have dreamed up with Cobb rampaging in her house.

It isn't a murder story. Cobb might very well just use her phone and bathroom, pocket a few trinkets and be on his demented way. The story as it stands now is more about sales technique than it is about crime. The environment of the story is our environment— the prime-time world of horrendous news stories. Cobb takes advantage of that paranoid context to promote the Cyclops. I've ladled on images of threat—symbols and metaphors—with obvious glee and little moderation, but they are only *images* of threat. Nothing happens beyond the sale of a five dollar door peeper.

There is very little in the way of plot here. There are no antecedent events of any importance to the story's development. (There is a sense of *impending* event, which provides the kind of suspense usually associated with crime stories. Charles Baxter's story "Through the Safety Net" derives its plot effects from an impending event that never quite happens: A psychic makes a dire prophecy about the principal character's life.) In "The Smile of a Turtle," we learn a little about Cobb—his somewhat peculiar training in sales technique—but we don't really know if he is a psychopathic monster or just a good, albeit quirky, salesman. The woman is a stock victim—her character is not developed. The story, then, is a moment (exaggerated considerably) of contemporary suburban life. More a chunk of life than a slice. A fat *trenche de vie*; a longish vignette.

Where did the idea for this story come from? When my wife and I were living in California, a salesman came by one day with a burlap bag full of door peepers. He had no sales technique. But they were cheap, and I, like all victims of the six o'clock news, felt I needed one. When he had drilled a hole in our hollow tract-house door and attached the peeper, he asked if he could use the phone. I let him. He was a harmless old guy with a limp.

The sea of stories laps at your door.

CLOSED-ENDED STORIES

If I have given the impression that the open-ended story is *by its nature* superior to the closed-ended story, I want to correct that notion now. No "type" of story is better by nature than any other. The writing is everything. Genius will produce great art regardless of the convention it works in.

Some of the greatest stories ever written are closed-ended. "The Short Happy Life of Francis Macomber" is as closed-ended as a story can get. Francis Macomber and his wife, Margot, are on a hunting safari in Africa, guided by the professionl hunter, Wilson. After Macomber wounds a lion, Wilson insists they must go into the tall grass to finish the animal off. The lion, hidden by the grass, now has the advantage: The hunters won't see it until they are practically on top of it. When the lion charges, Macomber bolts. Macomber is surprised and humiliated by his cowardice. But he makes up for it the next day while hunting cape buffalo, an animal easily as dangerous as the lion. This time Macomber stands his ground as a wounded buffalo charges him, only to be shot dead by his wife. The shooting will be regarded as accidental, but the reader understands that Macomber has been murdered. Because he has found his courage, courage that will change the course of his life, Margot realizes that she has lost control of him and that it will only be a matter of time now before he leaves her. (This thumbnail sketch of the story doesn't do justice to the psychosexual dynamics at its core. Read it if you haven't yet done so. The "sexual politics" of the story may be seen as outdated by some, but the story remains a masterpiece of the form.)

Hemingway slams the door *twice* on this story—the shooting of Macomber by his wife is then followed by Wilson's relentless needling of Margot until she breaks down. Bang, and then bang again. Nothing is left to the imagination of the reader.

Frank O'Connor's "Guests of the Nation" is another prime example of the closed-ended story. This story, while thin on plot, concludes its dramatic potential as completely as it does its thematic intention. It's a savage and tender story that breaks my heart every time I read it. (A pair of captured English soldiers await their fate at the hands of a few members of the Irish army. But during the long wait the "enemies"—through political and religious argument and card games—become friends. Then the word comes down from headquarters: The captured soldiers are to be shot.) It's the ultimate "man's inhumanity to man" story. As you read it, you sense that O'Connor knows that he's got hold of the major tragic situation of our century. Maybe of any century.

O'Connor won't let the story go. There's no way he could. He milks the story of every dramatic possibility, committing himself to broad, unsubtle strokes. He has a theme, and he paints it in foot-high letters. He risks the soapbox approach to fiction writing, he risks sentimentality. Yet it is one of the finest stories I have ever read.

7

FORM:
PASSIONATE VIRTUOSITY

A story should appear to be seamless even though it is crosshatched with stitchery. A seamless story progresses smoothly. There is a kinetic energy in it that needs to be maintained even though the story itself moves not only forward but backward and sometimes crablike to one side or the other. In spite of these nonlinear backward and sideways movements (flashbacks and digressions), the reader must keep the sensation that the entire structure is moving forward. This sense of progression is directly dependent on the story's form.

Form is the story's shape. By shape I mean two things. First, I mean the superficial, visible characteristics, such as the seemingly trivial elements that follow:

- sentence and paragraph length
- the use of white space between sections
- the absence of white space
- the absence of quotation marks in dialogue
- the uses of dashes instead of quotation marks
- the use of pictorial devices such as asterisks

Some stories, such as F. Scott Fitzgerald's "Winter Dreams," have numbered sections that act like minichapters. Henry James' "The Tree of Knowledge" also uses numbered minichapters. The novelist and short story writer Larry Brown wrote one of his stories in very short lines.

> The lines descend down the
> middle of the page like
> this for several pages
> yet command our attention
> —because of the form?
> Or for the story itself?

But form also consists of the more affective structural components, such as the narrating voice: Is the story told in first person, second person, third person, or combinations of these? The diction and vocabulary the narrating voice uses is an aspect of form that tells me a lot about what to expect as I read on. The voice in any Henry James story is instantly identifiable, as is the voice in any Hemingway story.

Point of view and point-of-view shifts, tense and tense shifts, how time functions in the story, the way the texture of the story's locale is rendered—all these contribute to a story's structure.

The sounds individual words make and the rhythms of strings of words—these are the heartbeats, the thrusts and hesitations within the form, and are part of the form.

Then there's the writer's tactics: The story might be told in a monologue, in a series of scenes, or in undramatized narrative. The writer might play with various devices of presentation: an exchange of letters, a message on an answering machine or in a bottle, a confession, an official report, a reconstructed fairy tale, a fable.

Though it's not very useful as a visual metaphor, I think of form as the vessel that contains the story—an abstract vessel of many dimensions. The shape of the vessel changes from story to story. Certain genre stories have more or less the same shape. Commercial stories—very nearly an oxymoron these days—take on the shape favored by the editorial policies of the magazines they are published in. (The genre romance novel has a form so rigidly specific that you can get detailed instructions on how to write one from the publishing firms that specialize in them.) Stories of literary quality find their own form.

It's easier to talk about form when the topic is poetry. There are a number of traditional forms, such as sonnets, villanelles, and sestinas, not to mention the other shaping elements of verse (including free verse), such as meter, syllables per line, line breaks, enjambment, diction, stanza size, and sometimes the poet's lung capacity—a line measured by the amount of syllables and caesuras the lungs can hold.

It's a little trickier to speak of form as it concerns the short story. The short story has no tradition of established forms (though it has its roots in its historical predecessors—the fable, the parable, the tale, and the sketch). We tinker, looking for the best way to get the story told. And the way it's told makes the story either compelling or tedious.

The nearly defunct method of writing commercial short stories—stories that have a clear beginning, a defined middle, and a recognizable end, and which are invested with conflict, rising action, complication, crisis, and resolution—is our only "conventional" form. But most contemporary writers have found this formulaic approach insufficient to their purposes. Form and content are interdependent, and the content of most contemporary short stories won't fit comfortably into this old pattern. In any case, it's a pattern that was more suited to the magazine fiction of fifty years ago that resulted in the "standardized product" the critic Kenneth Allan Robinson (mentioned in chapter one) vented his complaints about.

FINDING THE FORM

I had a story I wanted to write. My next-door neighbor Dora, a sweet old alcoholic, had a live-in boyfriend who was at least thirty years her junior. They were a friendly couple. We got along very well. Once a month or so, my wife would give Dora a loaf of fresh baked bread; now and then Dora would give my wife a newly crocheted doily. Dora's boyfriend, Charlie, was a timberjack on medical disability because of a bad accident. A tie chain on a lumber truck had snapped under heavy stress. The recoiling chain had whipped into Charlie's spine, breaking several vertebrae. He was living on workmen's compensation. It wasn't enough money for Charlie. He started intercepting Dora's Social Security checks. He forged her signature and cashed them, financing his own considerable drinking habit. When Dora discovered it was Charlie who'd been lifting her checks from her mailbox, she threw him out.

I'd just started writing short stories, and I wanted to write one based on characters like Dora and Charlie. I first tried to write it in a conventional way. I couldn't do it. *The way I was writing it falsified the story.* How could that be? I don't know, but it's true. Maybe I felt that Dora and Charlie's relationship was unconventional and so needed special treatment. I'm not convinced of that, but it makes sense. In any case, the story would not be told the way I set out to tell it—not with any energy or conviction at least. Maybe I believed my material really *was* conventional and that to exploit it well I had to find a unique method of expressing it. Again, that's just a speculation. The truth is, I was just up against a wall and needed to get over it somehow.

I was in a graduate school poetry workshop at the time and had been dealing with the idea of form as it applied to verse and so it was natural for me to transfer my preoccupation with form to the short story.

I find all this very mysterious. A story is a story, isn't it? No, it isn't. Not until you find the way of telling it. Not until you find its multidimensional *shape*. It was as if the story were withholding itself from me until I figured out how to tell it.

The writer Frederick Busch, in an interview, described the history of one of his short stories in this same way. The story was about the death of his grandfather. He originally wrote the story from the point of view of a thirteen-year-old. The story, for whatever reason, didn't work for Busch. A decade later, when he was a father himself, he wrote the story from the father's point of view. Suddenly the story came to life. It worked. Busch writes, "The answer was as simple and as elusive as that change in point of view, but when I made it I was finally able to tell the truth *more fully* about that father, son, and grandfather." (My italics.)

I can't explain this sort of thing very well, even to myself. The problem, I think, is one of having too many choices. A story can be told in hundreds of ways. The writer's dilemma is to find the single best one.

A student of mine wrote a story about a man whose wife is an agoraphobe. She is also phobic about dirt—she makes the kids wash their hands fifteen times a day, won't let anyone wear their street shoes in the house, keeps the furniture under double plastic covers, and so on. The story begins with a dialogue between the husband and the psychiatrist who is treating the man's wife. The psychiatrist takes the wife's side because he likes the wife and dislikes the husband. His unprofessional behavior is not challenged by the husband, and the reader is left to wonder why.

This dialogue goes on for about four pages. It is naked dialogue without attribution. The spoken words just hang in space, unamplified or biased by gesture. Then the story switches to first person, the point of view given to the husband. Suddenly the story leaps off the page. It comes to life—you can hear its rhythmic heart. We see the characters for the first time, sympathize with them and suffer for them. But then the writer ends the story back in the psychiatrist's office with a few more pages of naked dialogue. What had been given a brief life died again.

The story, *in the way it was written*, didn't work. The writer—like most beginning writers who have just finished their first drafts—couldn't immediately see why it wasn't working or what was needed to make it work. She wanted the story to retain the structure her intuition told her was going to be right for the story she had to tell. Others in the workshop told her to get rid of the psychologist, or at least embed truncated versions of those office scenes somewhere within the first-person narration.

The writer's intuition was wrong in this case, but it will be right in others. To her credit, she came to believe that what she had done was wrong—wrong because it wasn't getting the story told. She had a good story to tell, but the way she had chosen to tell it was undermining it. After she has been writing for a number of years, after having written hundreds of short stories, both good and bad, she will be able to intuit accurately the form a particular story needs. When she can't, she'll know to put it on a shelf and consign the work to her subconscious, which may, at some later date, hand her the solution.

I've put away stories I couldn't figure out for years before lightning struck. The brain and its fickle tenant, the mind, work in mysterious ways.

Back to Dora and Charlie: About the time I'd begun to think about their story as a possibility for fiction, I'd bought an anthology of recent Italian writing. In it was a short story about a couple suffering through the end of their love affair. A fairly ordinary story, except for the way it was being told. The writer had removed *time* from the story, thus defeating the "ordinariness" of the subject. It astonished me. How could she do that? Time is not some arbitrary device that can be used or not used. Time governs everything. Time, if not God, is God's taskmaster. *This* happens and then *that* happens. Every effect has its cause, and the cause *precedes* the effect. (Time, someone once said, is what prevents everything from happening at once.) There's no possible way you can remove chronology from a story. But she did. She twisted linear duration into a corkscrew. She stuffed distinct events into the pinprick of the corkscrew's tip and yet preserved their integrity. *Everything happened at once.* I hadn't by that time read anything by the great Argentine writer Jorge Luis Borges, who refuted (and played with) the notion of absolute time in his essays and in his fiction, but I suppose the Italian writer I wanted to emulate *had.* My attraction to the idea of undoing time was a secondary infection.

She impressed me. I was so impressed I stole her method. (T.S. Eliot: "Bad poets borrow, good poets steal." The same goes for short story writers. It saves you time. Eliot wasn't recommending plagiarism; he was talking about method.) I realized I could tell the story of Dora and Charlie in this way and not violate what I had come to understand about their relationship. This time-collapsing idea gave the story its form, and the form validated—for me—the story. I don't think you can write a story that isn't somehow validated for you by the way you choose to write it. If you try to write it in a way you hold suspect—for whatever reason—you might end up paralyzed with self-doubt or boredom, the words coming to you as grudgingly as blocks of granite dragged through a mealy bog.

Robert Wallace, in his book *Writing Poems*, puts it another way: "Form is valuable because it preserves content." This seemed to be the case with my story. I needed to find the form that would make the content give up its dark heart. I know that sounds dramatic and a bit overblown, but that's what I felt. Do I understand this? Not at all.

I wanted to make the story orbit an instant of time. It would go nowhere. It would have nowhere *to* go. "Going" requires duration. I would get rid of duration. Events would become free of time's treadmill. The narrative clock would stop. The characters would become fixed in an infinitesimal moment; they'd become figures in a frieze. And at the same time, the story would retain its kinetic energy and the illusion of forward progress.

Is it a good story? It's okay for a rank beginner. Did I succeed in my aims? I thought so at the time, but now I know the story fell short. My ambition exceeded my technical skill. I didn't fully understand the consequences of the method I'd chosen. Even so, the story was published in a small-circulation quarterly—payment in copies—and eventually picked up by an anthology. Not much of a story, no. But it was a breakthrough for me. I learned a lot from it. I learned how a realized form can get a story told in a way that excited me. I learned how form, like a lens, will keep a story focused.

It's easier to show you what I mean than talk abstractly about it. So here's that novice's story.

QUEEN

"Is it well done, is it cooked enough for you?" She looked over her shoulder at Page, who was seated at the table, chewing slowly, judging the meat. Evelyn looked over her shoulder again. "I asked is it well done, is it cooked enough?" Her five cats were moving between her swollen ankles, coaxing her. She tested the large beet to see if it was done. Her legs were aching again. Page fished in his mouth, pulled out a torn piece of tendon. He wiped his fingers on his pants. He took another beer from the six-pack at his feet, removed the cap, drank deeply. She had annoyed him and he had announced, "No, she's no mother, but she's a welfare queen just the same." He regretted saying it. He'd meant it as a joke and had snorted loudly in self-appreciation. Evelyn drank sweet port out of a water glass, and in the bar where he had said it, she began to cry. She put her head against Page's shoulder and moaned over and over, louder each time, and Page felt compelled to shrug hard against her face until she stopped. Some at the bar smiled tolerantly, others bent to their drinks. She was near seventy and her heart was not good. The port, or sometimes the sherry, gave her strength. She was proud of her strong hands and she shook the hands of workingmen up and down the bar. She had good hands and liked to display them. The flesh was falling in her face and she was known as a character. She had never married. For years she had lived alone in a little house by the railroad bridge on the edge of Cutter Creek. The creek is full and green and explosive against big rocks in the spring, but by late summer it is nothing more than a trickle, studded with rusty cans. Evelyn looked over her shoulder and watched Page chewing slowly, reflectively. He was squinting, neck stiff, as he judged the meat. She had annoyed him. The hard veins in the backs of her knees ached. He had robbed her once, taking the welfare money, and she had forgiven him. It's all right, she said, you needed it. He meant it as a joke, but wound up spending it all. She tested the large beet to see if it was done. A log train carrying ponderosa made the small house jump. The dishes in the cupboard clattered. The train's slow rhythm rocked the floor. "Is it cooked enough for you?" Page searched the crevices of his teeth with his tongue, drank deeply from the tall brown bottle. He had regretted saying it, but the regret was dim in his mind now. He chewed the piece of meat slowly, judging it. He said it again in the cab on the way home. "No, she's no mother. She's a queen just the same." He left out the meanness this time. He left out the joke. He said it with tenderness, her head against his shoulder, her hand tightening on his. "Don't shrug me off." In the bar her hoarse sobbing was loud and inconsolable. It grew until the sly sound of death crept into it. He shrugged hard against her face until she stopped. Some in the bar smiled tolerantly. In the cab she whimpered demurely with an ageless femininity. She dabbed her puffed eyes on a small silk hankie painted with wild flowers. She was much older than Page, who was only forty-three. They had been close friends for years and had seen happier days together before Evelyn's health had deteriorated. Page knew she could not live much longer. Her heart would often leave her legs and fingers numb or cramped with pain. It was on these occasions that she would coax Page to rub her feet and then her hands and arms. And Page would often agree, usually after explaining that he had some errands to run first, some people to see. Page had quit logging years ago. A tie chain on a lumber truck had snapped, splintering three vertebrae high in his back. The rolling rhythm of the log train sent a memory of pain into his neck. He knew he'd had to say it again in the cab, and said it firmly. Tenderly, but with masculine dignity. Earlier he'd meant it as a joke. The cabdriver had turned his head but not completely, then glanced in the rearview mirror. Page knew this would happen but he said it again, anyway, "No, she's no mother." Then he paused, making both the cabdriver and Evelyn stop to listen. Then he said, "But she's a queen, just the same." Evelyn turned from the stove, her eyes swallowed by their surrounding flesh, her flesh sweating through the rosy makeup. "Is it well done, is it cooked enough?" Page's mouth was full. He swished the remaining beer until it was milky in the brown bottle. He glanced up at Evelyn, raised his eyebrows as if to speak, but only a soft belch murmured in his throat. He drank the remaining beer, giving moisture to the mass of meat and bread still in his mouth. Evelyn's five cats rubbed against her thick legs, some rising slightly, their pink mouths begging. He had taken her welfare money once, but she had forgiven him. You needed it, Page. It was a joke, he said. But he'd spent it all. She tested the large beet to see if it was done. Page fished in his mouth, pulled out a torn piece of tendon. In the cab she said her legs were gone. The driver looked back, impatient to end the afternoon shift. Page watched her knuckles turn white against the pink hankie painted with yellow, blue, and purple wild flowers. Page said, "Ten years ago I was thirty-three." The cabdriver and Evelyn looked at Page. The slow meter ticked then stopped. The driver and Page helped Evelyn into the house. She was heavy with age and they entered sideways, the driver, Evelyn, then Page. They eased her down into the couch and she sank into its faded tapestry, sighing, then coughing. The sly sound of death creaked in her chest. Page paid the driver and the man left, letting the screen door slam. There had been an alarming moment for Page when Evelyn seemed lifeless. Her head rested on the back of the couch. Her mouth was open. Her eyes were dim and fixed on distance. Page heard a thin rasping in her chest. He recalled the rasp of chain saws in the trees far away. Evelyn pushed a fork into the large beet. She looked over her shoulder at Page. Her cats rubbed against her legs, tails up and quivering. Page looked up from his food, squinting. She had annoyed him. He swished the remaining beer until it was milky in the brown bottle. He regretted saying it. He had never said anything like it before. And when Evelyn asked him to do her legs he had said yes he would and that he had nothing else to do that was important. She looked at him, the thin rasping in her breast gone, her pale eyes small and liquid. The stinging haze of chip burners was in the room. He knelt and removed her shoes.

Her feet were splotched and swollen. The old toes yellowing. Evelyn leaned back into the faded tapestry and closed her eyes. Her face relaxed into an ageless femininity. It was the end of summer. The house retained the day's heat and would do so through the night. The thin ribbon of water that was Cutter Creek made sly talking sounds against the large stones that lined its bed. The air was heavy and did not move. "I asked, is it well done, is it cooked enough for you?" Page searched the crevices of his teeth with his tongue. He squinted, his neck stiff, as he judged the meat. He drank the white beer. He regretted saying it. He'd never said anything like it before. And when she asked him to do her legs he said yes. His hands were hard from years of logging and he worked her veined calves with great gentleness. Evelyn leaned back into the stuffed cushions and closed her eyes. A chain saw somewhere rasped. She reached out and touched his head and her fingers went into his hair. She was proud of the strength in her hands. She had good hands and liked to display them. She shook the hands of workingmen up and down the bar. She was known as a character. Some at the bar smiled tolerantly, some bent closer to their drinks. She closed her fingers on Page's hair and brought his face down slowly to her lap. Page made soft murmuring sounds. You're a sly one, she said, without anger. His neck was stiff. Evelyn looked over at Page, then tested the large beet to see if it was done. Her five cats moved between her legs, coaxing. She had annoyed him and he had said something he now regretted. Evelyn brought his face down slowly to her lap. Page gripped the backs of her knees and worked the hard knots of blue veins. Evelyn looked over her shoulder at Page. Page was seated at the table. He had robbed her once. It had been a joke. You're sly, she said. He fished in his mouth and pulled out a torn piece of tendon. She had good hands. She liked to display them. "Don't you shrug me off." Her fingers moved willfully in his hair. He had never said any-thing like it before. It's all right, you needed it, she said. She looked over her shoulder at Page. Page glanced up. He swished the beer until it was milky. "Is it well done, is it cooked enough for you?"

Time's arrow doubles back on itself and makes a loop by the use of refrain lines, the major refrain being, "Is it well done, is it cooked enough for you?" The story is told in a single paragraph with no conspicuous transitions, which imparts momentum to an essentially static field of action. The divisions between incidents are consequently blurred.

It was my first experiment with form. It didn't quite do what I wanted it to do. The divisions between incidents are not so much blurred as they are railroaded past the reader's notice by narrative speed. By doing this, I hoped to give the impression that time had been collapsed and thus eliminated from the narrative.

I was wrong. Language is time based. As soon as I wrote, "She had annoyed him and he had announced, 'No, she's no mother, but she's a welfare queen just the same,' " I had produced a flashback—the first of several—taking the reader back to the bar where Dora and Charlie had gotten drunk. The use of the past-perfect tense undermined the method I thought I was using. Chronology entered the story every time I wrote "he had," "she had," and so on. In spite of my intentions, I was falling back on time-dependent narrative technique. But the story was published anyway. Luckily the editor who accepted it didn't know (and most likely wouldn't have cared anyway) what I'd been up to and how I'd failed. He just liked the story for its own sake.

The Italian story that had inspired me did a far better job of keeping the action bottled up in the moment. It didn't have to pro-vide—as "Queen" does—miniflashbacks to account for the situa-tion the lovers find themselves in. It was a good lesson for me though. The lesson is this: When you decide on a particular form, you need to exploit it boldly and completely. To do this, you need to know its *rules*. If you fail to understand its requirements and possibilities, elements from your cache of hackneyed story motifs will exert themselves. They will undermine your bold effort.

What do I mean by a form's "rules"? Nothing more than the limits and liberties it allows. Whenever you sit down to write, you give yourself rules of procedure. You may not realize this right away, but somewhere during the composition of your story, you have to decide what is allowable and what is not. For example, in "The Smile of a Turtle," I knew, at some point or other during composition, that the point of view would be restricted to Cobb, that the story would be told in present tense to give it a sense of immediacy and to keep the possibility of threat imminent, and that the language would have velocity as well as an overt brutality to it. These were the "rules." They gave limits to what I could do and, within those limits, the freedom to exploit the subject fully. To know these limits and freedoms, you have to understand the form completely.

Here's an example of how not understanding the rules of a form can undermine your efforts. A student of mine wanted to use the "diary form" to tell a story. She thought that by having her character record her most private thoughts about the situation she was involved in she could achieve an honesty and directness beyond the possibilities of ordinary narrative. With some misgivings, I agreed. The diary form can be powerful—whether the diarist is uncomfortably honest or is self-deceived and therefore an unreliable witness to his or her own life. Fascinating notions. However, I think it's a severely limiting form, loaded with pitfalls. But I'm not one to discourage anyone's moment of inspiration.

My student's "diary" opened with a commonplace entry, which was fine. But as the entries began to reflect the dramatic situation, they became more and more like straightforward fiction—complete with scenes, lengthy descriptions, and even flashbacks. No one writes a diary that way. She had violated the form she had chosen because it was too constricting; without understanding why, she lost faith in it. I suggested that she read some great literary diaries, such as *A Writer's Diary*, by Virginia Woolf, if she still wanted to proceed this way. Woolf's diary is book-length, but even so, there is much to learn about the style of the diarist from it. I also asked her to read "If I

Should Open My Mouth," a story by Paul Bowles written in the form of a diary. It's the story of a personality revealed in spite of itself. The diary form is wonderfully suited to this tactic. I also recommended Joyce Carol Oates' story "How I Contemplated the World From the Detroit House of Correction and Began My Life Over Again," subtitled, "Notes for an Essay for an English Class at Baldwin Country Day School; Poking Around in Debris; Disgust and Curiosity; a Revelation of the Meaning of Life; a Happy Ending . . ." It's not exactly a diary, but closely related to it in form and method, and, as such, a good story to study in order to understand how flexible this form can be within its severe constraints.

FORM AND CONTENT

To get an idea how form can not only determine how a story is told but become part of the story's meaning, read Robert Coover's "The Babysitter," (included in his collection titled *Pricksongs and Descants*) a dazzling tour de force that mixes reality, fantasy, and wish-fulfilling daydreams in a mischievous montage that shifts point of view with reckless abandon. Time's smooth continuum is lovingly segmented. Narrative is diced into packets of quanta. And yet the story has a recognizable progression, from the superficial order and good behavior of suburbia to the libidinal chaos locked in its heart. Coover puts a big arrhythmia in time's plodding pulse while the story spins away in adrenalized nonlinearity. The story is related to cubism in art, where all dimensional perspectives are rendered in one plane.

Why write this way? Why wrench stories into shapes that are unrecognizable to the average law-abiding citizen? Robert Scholes, in his book of critical essays *Fabulation and Metafiction*, summarizes the argument: "The artist who wants to capture modern life . . . must care for form, because only appropriately new forms will be capable of representing modern life." The realists of the late nineteenth century were influenced by Darwinism as well as unprecedented advances in physical science, advances that eclipsed myth and mystery. The modernists of the early twentieth century were

121

influenced by Freudian psychology, Einsteinian physics, and all the great leaps in technology, such as radio, heavier-than-air flight, television, and the weapons of mass destruction. What worked in the literary arts of 1868 might not work so well in 1918.

Contemporary writers are similarly influenced by quantum physics, string theory, microbiology, genetic research, new theories of cognition, and psychopharmacology. Writers don't work in a cultural vacuum. Their antennae are long and sensitive. What they are exposed to can't help but find a direct channel into their fiction—not just as subject matter but in the very way fiction is structured. Jackson Pollock said an artist can't, in the age of atomic bombs, paint the kind of picture that was painted during the Renaissance.

The form you choose puts each sentence you write to this test: Does this sentence add to or detract from the organizing principle of the story? Form makes you walk a well-defined path. Does this inhibit creativity? Not at all. T.S. Eliot once suggested in an essay that the strictures of form (paradoxically) liberate the imagination. The problems that form presents are purely technical. The part of the brain that seizes the opportunity to solve problems is also the part that interferes with creativity. It is the "censor," the "critic," that worries about every irrational impulse the imagination is subject to. But without these irrational impulses (also know as intuition, insight, and inspiration), there can be no creativity. Form distracts the censor with a technical problem while the irrational engines of creativity rev up. Recent studies of right-brain and left-brain function support this notion.

I am no literary critic and therefore won't attempt to discuss the theoretical aspects of form. Formalism was a movement in twentieth-century literature that promoted the aesthetic aspects of writing over its perceived social responsibility. It began in Russia in the 1920s where it was subsequently banned by the Communist Party. Then it spread to the West. Borges, when asked if literature shouldn't justify itself by engaging contemporary social and political issues, said, "I think it is engaged all the time. We don't have to worry about that. Being contemporaries, we have to write in the style and mode of our times. If I write a story—even about the man in the moon—it would be an Argentine story, because I'm an Argentine; and it would fall back on Western civilization because that's the civilization I belong to." He gives as an example Flaubert's novel *Salambo*, which Flaubert called a Carthaginian novel, ". . . but anyone can see it was written by a 19th century French realist. . . . I don't think you should try to be loyal to your century or your opinions, because you are being loyal to them all the time." In the same way, I think it is equally true that most contemporary short story writers have inherited the precepts of formalism as well, whether they know it or not.

For my part, I think of form in a purely utilitarian way. I need to write my stories in ways that draw out their possibilities, and finding the right form does that for me. Even if a story has in it a polemic born of some socially responsible impulse, its form still is a major factor in its success as a *story*.

USING FORM

There was an article in our local newspaper about an accidental spraying of herbicide. The spraying helicopter dumped its load of poison on the wrong farm. Weeks later, odd things began to happen on this farm. The animals got sick. Some behaved strangely. The cows acted insane, as did the pigs. A horse wandered into the next county. Chickens tried to fly even as they were dying. The farmer and his wife and their children developed symptoms similar to those exhibited by nerve gas victims. I was moved to write a story about this incident. I struggled with the idea for a while, trying to render the situation in realistic terms. It didn't work. What realistic picture could I draw about a poisoned farm? That kind of story would ultimately have to be about the people who live on that farm, their relationships, their states of mind. The accidental spraying of herbicide would have to be nothing more than an incident in their lives that either complicated or simplified whatever *other* conflicts they had to deal with. I didn't want to write a story in which the thing that had initially excited my interest was reduced to a dramatic catalyst for some domestic drama. No! I wanted to make a strong environmental statement! I was riding the high horse of righteousness! (Yes, I *was* thinking in terms of theme before I had put one word on paper—the very thing I warned you against in chapter four! I didn't say—did I?—that I always follow my own advice.)

This was back in the early 1970s, and the general mood was apocalyptic. Things seemed to be going to hell. In any case, I didn't know any farmers, didn't have the kind of grasp of the farming life a realistic story would have required. I decided to give it up. I knew the story I wanted to write would make some kind of political statement. I also knew I wasn't the kind of writer who was comfortable using fiction as a platform for social commentary.

Then I had an inspiration: "Jack and the Beanstalk" came to my rescue. This was the form I was looking for. The fairy tale form gave me two things I needed:

1. freedom from the tunnel vision of theme
2. freedom to explore other aspects of the relationships between the characters, aspects suggested by, but not explored in, the old fairy tale

Bruno Bettelheim's book *The Uses of Enchantment* was a valuable reference work. Bettelheim examines the hidden psychological meanings in Grimm's fairy tales—the original Grimm's, not the less savage Disney versions we read to our kids. It's a valuable sourcebook for writers. It turns out, according to Bettelheim, that these ancient stories (many of which go back thousands of years) record the universal constants of human psychology. They were not tales to entertain children. These were folk tales, meant to be heard by the entire community. They were entertaining, but they also dramatized the emotional conflicts every human being experiences from early childhood on.

My story would still make a strong environmental statement, but it would be embedded now in a story about the relationships between the mother; her son, Jack; the old man with the magic seeds; and the giant, Big Pete Parley—the successful farmer who intends to marry Jack's mother. If Parley represents the forces of agricultural progress, then Jack (in his sullen Oedipal rage) is the anti-establishment hero bent on sabotaging Parley's plans.

This approach solved my problem. Not the problem of writing the story—that had to be sweated out word by word—but the problem of *how* to tell it and what shape to give it. And it took me off the dangerous path of writing a one-note story with a monotonous thematic message.

The resulting story, "Weeds," *can* be seen as an ecological warning, the magic (mutant) seeds not resulting in a towering beanstalk but in a plague of hellish weeds that take over the countryside. But it can also be seen as a Hamlet-style revenge tale: The father is killed by the forces of agricultural progress—represented by Big Pete Parley—and Jack (as a bumpkin Hamlet) seeks justice at any cost. Finding the form for "Weeds" made it great fun to write.

WEEDS

A black helicopter flapped out of the morning sun and dumped its sweet orange mist on our land instead of the Parley farm where it was intended. It was weedkiller, something strong enough to wipe out leafy spurge, knapweed, and Canadian thistle, but it made us sick.

My father had a fatal stroke a week after that first spraying. I couldn't hold down solid food for nearly a month and went from 200 pounds to 170 in that time. Mama went to bed and slept for two days, and when she woke up she was not the same. She'd lost something of herself in that long sleep, and something that wasn't herself had replaced it.

Then it hit the animals. We didn't have much in the way of animals, but one by one they dropped. The chickens, the geese, the two old mules—Doc and Rex—and last of all, our only cow, Miss Milky, who was more or less the family pet.

Miss Milky was the only animal that didn't outright up and die. She just got sick. There was blood in her milk and her milk was thin. Her teats got so tender and brittle that she would try to mash me against the milk stall wall when I pulled at them. The white part of her eyes looked like fresh meat. Her piss was so strong that the green grass wherever she stood died off. She got so bound up that when she'd lift her tail and bend with strain, only one black apple would drop. Her breath took on a burning sulfurous stink that would make you step back.

She also went crazy. She'd stare at me like she all at once had a desperate human mind and had never seen me before. Then she'd act as if she wanted to slip a horn under my ribs and peg me to the barn. She would drop her head and charge, blowing like a randy bull, and I would have to scramble out of the way. Several times I saw her gnaw on her hooves or stand stock-still in water up to her blistered teats. Or she would walk backward all day long, mewling like a lost cat that had been dropped off in a strange place. That mewling was enough to make you want to clap a set of noise dampers on your ears. The awful sound led Mama to say this: "It's the death song of the land, mark my words."

Mama never talked like that before in her life. She'd always been a cheerful woman who could never see the bad part of anything that was at least fifty percent good. But now she was dark and careful as a gypsy. She would have spells of derangement during which she'd make noises like a wild animal, or she'd play the part of another person— the sort of person she'd normally have nothing to do with at all. At Daddy's funeral she got dressed up in an old and tattered evening gown the color of beet juice, her face painted and powdered like that of a barfly. And while the preacher told the onlookers what a fine man Daddy had been, Mama cupped her hands under her breasts and lifted them high, as if offering to appease a dangerous stranger. Then, ducking her head, she chortled, "Loo, loo, loo," her scared eyes scanning the trees for owls.

I was twenty-eight years old and my life had come to

nothing. I'd had a girl but I'd lost her through neglect and a careless attitude that had spilled over into my personal life, souring it. I had no ambition to make something worthwhile of myself and it nettled her. Toward the end she began to parrot her mother: "You need to get yourself *established*, Jack," she would say. But I didn't want to get myself established. I was getting poorer and more aimless day by day. I supposed she believed that "getting established" would put a stop to my downhill slide but I had no desire to do whatever it took to accomplish that.

Shortly after Daddy died, the tax man came to our door with a paper in his hand. "Inheritance tax," he said, handing me the paper.

"What do you mean?" I asked.

"It's the law," he said. "Your father died, you see. And that's going to cost you some. You should have made better plans." He tapped his forehead with his finger and winked. He had a way of expressing himself that made me think he was country born and raised but wanted to seem citified. Or maybe it was the other way around.

"I don't understand this," I mumbled. I felt the weight of a world I'd so far been able to avoid. It was out there, tight-assed and squinty-eyed, and it knew to the dollar and dime what it needed to keep itself in business.

"Simple," he said. "Pay or move off. The government is the government and it can't bend a rule to accommodate the confused. It's your decision. Pay or the next step is litigation."

He smiled when he said good-bye. I closed the door against the weight of his smile, which was the weight of the world. I went to a window and watched him head back to his government green car. The window was open and I could hear him. He was singing loudly in a fine tenor voice. He raised his right hand to hush an invisible audience that had broken into uncontrolled applause. I could still hear him singing as he slipped the car into gear and idled away. He was singing "Red River Valley."

Even though the farm was all ours, paid up in full, we had to give the government $7000 for the right to stay on it. The singing tax man said we had inherited the land from my father, and the law was sharp on the subject.

I didn't know where the money was going to come from. I didn't talk it over with Mama because even in her better moments she would talk in riddles. To a simple question such as, "Should I paint the barns this year, Mama?" she might answer, "I've no eyes for glitter, nor ears for their ridicule."

One day I decided to load Miss Milky into the stock trailer and haul her into Saddle Butte where the vet, Doc Nevers, had his office. Normally, Doc Nevers would come out to your place but he'd heard about the spraying that was going on and said he wouldn't come within three miles of our property until they were done.

The Parley farm was being sprayed regularly, for they grew an awful lot of wheat and almost as much corn and they had the biggest haying operation in the county. Often the helicopters they used were upwind from us and we were sprayed too. ("Don't complain," said Big Pete Parley when I called him up about it. "Think of it this way—you're getting your place weeded for free!" When I said I might have to dynamite some stumps on the property line and that he might get a barn or two blown away for free, he just laughed like hell, as if I had told one of the funniest jokes he'd ever heard.)

There was a good windbreak between our places, a thick grove of lombardy poplars, but the orange mist, sweet as a flower garden in spring bloom, sifted through the trees and settled on our field. Soon the poplars were mottled and dying. Some branches curled in an upward twist, as if flexed in pain, and others became soft and fibrous as if the wood were trying to turn itself into sponge.

With Miss Milky in the trailer, I sat in the truck sipping on a pint of Lewis and Clark bourbon and looking out across our unplanted fields. It was late—almost too late—to plant anything. Mama, in the state she was in, hadn't even noticed.

In the low hills on the north side of the property, some ugly looking things were growing. From the truck they looked like white pimples on the smooth brown hill. Up close they were big as melons. They were some kind of fungus and they pushed up through the ground like the bald heads of fat babies. They gave off a rotten meat stink. I would get chillbumps just looking at them and if I touched one my stomach would rise. The bulbous heads had purple streaks on them that looked like blood vessels. I half expected to one day see human eyes clear the dirt and open. Big pale eyes that would see me and carry my image down to their deepest root. I was glad they seemed to prefer the hillside and bench and not the bottom land.

Justified or not, I blamed the growth of this fungus on the poison spray, just as I blamed it for the death of my father, the loss of our animals, and the strangeness of my mother. Now the land itself was becoming strange. And I thought, what about me? How am I being rearranged by that weedkiller?

I guess I should have gotten mad, but I didn't. Maybe I *had* been changed by the spray. Where once I had been a quick-to-take-offense hothead, I was now docile and thoughtful. I could sit on a stump and think for hours, enjoying the slow and complicated intertwinings of my own thoughts. Even though I felt sure the cause of all our troubles had fallen out of the sky, I would hold arguments with myself, as if there were always two sides to every question. If I said to myself, "Big Pete Parley has poisoned my family and farm and my father is dead because of it," I would follow it up with, "but Daddy was old anyway, past seventy-five and he always had high blood pressure. Anything could have touched off his stroke, from a wasp bite to a sonic boom."

"And what about Mama?" I would ask. "Senile with grief," came the quick answer. "Furthermore, Daddy himself used poison in his time. Cyanide traps for coyotes, DDT for mosquito larvae, arsenic for rats."

My mind was always doubling back on itself in this way and it would often leave me standing motionless in a field for hours, paralyzed with indecision, sighing like a moonstruck girl of twelve. I imagined myself mistaken by passersby for a scarecrow.

Sometimes I saw myself as a human weed, useless to other people in general and maybe harmful in some weedy way. The notion wasn't entirely unpleasant. Jack Hucklebone: a weed among the well-established money crops of life.

On my way to town with Miss Milky, I crossed over the irrigation ditch my father had fallen into with the stroke that killed him. I pulled over onto the shoulder and switched off the engine. It was a warm, insect-loud day in early June. A spray of grasshoppers clattered over the hood of the truck. June bugs ticked past the windows like little flying clocks. The thirteen-year locusts were back and raising a whirring hell. I was fifteen the last time they came but I didn't remember them arriving in such numbers. I expected more helicopters to come flapping over with special sprays meant just for them, even though they would be around for only a few weeks and the damage they would do is not much more than measurable. But anything that looks like it might have an appetite for a money crop brings down the spraying choppers. I climbed out of the truck and looked up into the bright air. A lone jet, eastbound, too high to see or hear, left its neat chalk line across the top of the sky. The sky itself was hot blue wax, north to south. A fat hammerhead squatted on the west horizon. It looked like a creamy oblong planet that had slipped its orbit and was now endangering the earth.

There's where Daddy died. Up the ditch about fifty yards

from here. I found him, buckled, white as paper, half under water. His one good eye, his right (he'd lost the left one thirty years ago when a tractor tire blew up in his face as he was filling it), was above water and wide open, staring at his hand as if it could focus on the thing it gripped. He was holding on to a root. He had big hands, strong, with fingers like thick hardwood dowels, but now they were soft and puffy, like the hands of a giant baby. Water bugs raced against the current toward him. His body blocked the ditch and little eddies swirled around it. The water bugs skated into the eddies and, fighting to hold themselves still in the roiling current, touched his face. They held still long enough to satisfy their curiosity, then slid back into the circular flow as if bemused by the strangeness of dead human flesh.

I started to cry, remembering it, thinking about him in the water, he had been so sure and strong, but then—true to my changed nature—I began to laugh at the memory, for his wide blue eye had had a puzzled cast to it, as if it had never before seen such an oddity as the ordinary root in his forceless hand. It was an expression he never wore in life.

"It was only a weed, Daddy," I said, wiping the tears from my face.

The amazed puzzlement stayed in his eye until I brushed down the lid.

Of course he had been dead beyond all talk and puzzlement. Dead when I found him, dead for hours, bloated dead. And this is how *I've* come to be—blame the spray or don't: the chores don't get done on time, the unplanted fields wait, Mama wanders in her mind, and yet I'll sit in the shade of my truck sipping on Lewis and Clark bourbon, inventing the thoughts of a dead man.

Time bent away from me like a tail-dancing rainbow. It was about to slip the hook. I wasn't trying to hold it. Try to hold it and it gets all the more slippery. Try to let it go and it sticks like a cocklebur to cotton. I was drifting somewhere between the two kinds of not trying: not trying to hold anything, not trying to let anything go.

Then he sat down next to me. The old man.

"You got something for me?" he said.

He was easily the homeliest man I had ever seen. His bald head was bullet-shaped and his lumpy nose was warty as a crookneck squash. His little, close-set eyes sat on either side of that nose like hard black beans. He had shaggy eyebrows that climbed upward in a white and wiry tangle. There was a blue lump in the middle of his forehead the size of a pullet's egg, and his hairy ear lobes touched his grimy collar. He was mumbling something, but it could have been the noise of the ditch water as it sluiced through the culvert under the road.

He stank of whiskey and dung, and looked like he'd been sleeping behind barns for weeks. His clothes were rags and he was caked with dirt from fingernail to jaw. His shoes were held together with strips of burlap. He untied some of these strips and took off his shoes. Then he slid his gnarled, corn-crusted feet into the water. His eyes fluttered shut and he let out a hissing moan of pleasure. His toes were long and twisted, the arthritic knuckles painfully bright. They reminded me of the surface roots of a stunted oak that had been trying to grow in hardpan. Though he was only about five feet tall, his feet were huge. Easy size twelves, wide as paddles.

He quit mumbling, cleared his throat, spit. "You got anything for me?" he said.

I handed him my pint. He took it, held it up to the sunlight, looked through the rusty booze as if testing for its quality.

"If it won't do," I said, "I could run into town to get something a little smoother for you. Maybe you'd like some Canadian Club or some twelve-year-old Scotch. I could run into town and be back in less than an hour. Maybe you'd like me to bring back a couple of fried chickens and a sack of buttered rolls." This was my old self talking, the hothead. But I didn't feel mad at him and was just being mouthy out of habit.

"No need to do that," he said, as if my offer had been made in seriousness. He took a long pull off my pint. "This snake piss is just fine by me, son." He raised the bottle to the sunlight again, squinted through it.

I wandered down the ditch again to the place where Daddy died. There was nothing there to suggest a recent dead man had blocked the current. Everything was as it always was. The water surged, the quick water bugs skated up and down inspecting brown clumps of algae along the banks, underwater weeds waved like slim snakes whose tails had been staked to the mud. I looked for the thistle he'd grabbed on to. I guess he thought that he was going to save himself from drowning by hanging on to its root, not realizing that the killing flood was *inside* his head. But there were many roots along the bank and none of them seemed more special than any other.

Something silver glinted at me. It was a coin. I picked it out of the slime and polished it against my pants. It was a silver dollar, a real one. It could have been his. He carried a few of the old cartwheels around with him for luck. The heft and gleam of the old silver coin choked me up.

I walked back to the old man. He had stuffed his bindle under his head for a pillow and had dozed off. I uncapped the pint and finished it, then flipped it into the weeds. It hit a rock and popped. The old man grunted and his eyes snapped open. He let out a barking snort and his black eyes darted around fiercely, like the eyes of a burrow animal caught in a daylight trap. Then, remembering where he was, he calmed down.

"You got something for me?" he asked. He pushed himself up to a sitting position. It was a struggle for him.

"Not any more," I said. I sat down next to him. Then,

from behind us, a deep groan cut loose. It sounded like siding being pried off a barn with a crow bar. We both turned to look at whatever had complained so mightily.

It was Miss Milky, up in the trailer, venting her misery. I'd forgotten about her. Horseflies were biting her. Black belts of them girdled her teats. Her red eyes peered sadly out at us through the bars. The corners of her eyes were swollen, giving her a Chinese look.

With no warning at all, a snapping hail fell on us. Only it wasn't hail. It was a moving cloud of thirteen-year locusts. They darkened the sky and they covered us. The noise was like static on the radio, miles of static across the bug-peppered sky, static that could drown out all important talk and idle music no matter how powerful the station.

The old man's face was covered with the bugs and he was saying something to me but I couldn't make out what it was. His mouth opened and closed, opened and closed. When it opened he'd have to brush away the locusts from his lips. They were like ordinary grasshoppers, only smaller, and they had big red eyes that seemed to glow with their own hellish light. Then, as fast as they had come, they were gone, scattered back into the fields. A few hopped here and there, but the main cloud had broken up.

I just sat there brushing at the lingering feel of them on my skin and trying to readjust myself to uncluttered air but my ears were still crackling with their racket.

The old man pulled at my sleeve, breaking me out of my daydream or trance. "You got something for me?" he asked.

I felt blue. Worse than blue. Sick. I felt incurable—ridden with the pointlessness of just about everything you could name. The farm struck me as a pointless wonder and I found the idea depressing and fearsome. Pointless bugs lay waiting in the fields for the pointless crops as the pointless days and seasons ran on and on into the pointless forever.

"Shit," I said.

"I'll take that worthless cow off your hands, then," said

the old man. "She's done for. All you have to do is look at her."

He didn't seem so old or so wrecked to me now. He was younger and bigger somehow, as if all his clocks had started running backwards, triggered by the locust cloud. He stood up. He looked thick across the shoulders like he'd done hard work all his life and could still do it. He showed me his right hand. It was yellow with hard calluses. His beady black eyes were quick and lively in their shallow sockets. The blue lump on his forehead glinted in the sun. It seemed deliberately polished as if it were an ornament. He took a little silver bell out of his pocket and rang it for no reason at all.

"Let me have her," he said.

"You want Miss Milky?" I asked. I felt weak and childish. Maybe I was drunk. My scalp itched and I scratched it hard. He rang his little silver bell again. I wanted to have it but he put it back into his pocket. Then he knelt down and opened his bindle. He took out a paper sack.

I looked inside. It was packed with seeds of some kind. I ran my fingers through them and did not feel foolish. I heard a helicopter putt-putting in the distance. I'll say this in defense of what I did: I knew Miss Milky was done for. Doc Nevers would have told me to shoot her. I don't think she was even good for hamburger. Old cow meat can sometimes make good hamburger but Miss Milky looked wormy and lean. And I wouldn't have trusted her bones for soup. The poison that had wasted her flesh and ruined her udder had probably settled in her marrow.

And so I unloaded my dying cow. He took out his silver bell again and tied it to a piece of string. He tied the string around Miss Milky's neck. Then he led her away. She was docile and easy as though this was exactly the way things were supposed to turn out.

My throat was dry. I felt too tired to move. I watched their slow progress down the path that ran along the ditch.

They got smaller and smaller until, against a dark hedge of box elders, they disappeared. I strained to see after them, but it was as if the earth had given them refuge, swallowing them into its deep, loamy, composting interior. The only sign that they still existed in the world was the tinkling of the silver bell he had tied around Miss Milky's neck. It was a pure sound, naked on the air.

Then a breeze opened a gap in the box elders and a long blade of sunlight pierced through them, illuminating and magnifying the old man and his cow, as if the air between us had formed itself into a giant lens. The breeze let up and the box elders shut off the sun again and I couldn't see anything but a dense quiltwork of black and green shadows out of which a raven big as an eagle flapped. It cawed in raucous good humor as it veered over my head.

I went on into town anyway, cow or no cow, and hit some bars. I met a girl from the East in the Hobble who thought I was a cowboy and I didn't try to correct her mistaken impression for it proved a free pass to good times.

When I got home Mama had company. She was dressed up in her beet juice gown and her face was powdered white. Her dark lips looked like a wine stain in snow but her clear blue eyes were direct and calm. There was no distraction in them.

"Hi, boy," said the visitor. It was Big Pete Parley. He was wearing a blue suit, new boots, a gray felt Stetson. He had a toothy grin on his fat red face.

I looked at Mama. "What's *he* want?" I asked. Something was wrong. I could feel it but I couldn't see it. It was Mama, the way she had composed herself maybe, or the look in her eyes, or her whitened skin. Maybe she had gone all the way insane. She went over to Parley and sat next to him on the davenport. She had slit her gown and it fell away from her thigh, revealing the veiny flesh.

"We're going to be married," she said. "Pete's tired of being a widower. He wants a warm bed."

As if to confirm it was no fantasy dreamed up by her senile mind, Big Pete slid his hand into the slit dress and squeezed her thigh. He clicked his teeth and winked at me.

"Pete knows how to run a farm," said Mama. "And you do not, Jackie." She didn't intend for it to sound mean or critical. It was just a statement of the way things were. I couldn't argue with her.

I went into the kitchen. Mama followed me in. I opened a beer. "I don't mean to hurt your feelings, Jackie," she said.

"He's scheming to get our land," I said. "He owns half the county, but that isn't enough."

"No," she said. "I'm the one who's scheming. I'm scheming for my boy who does not grasp the rudiments of the world."

I had the sack of seeds with me. I realized that I'd been rattling them nervously.

"What do you have there?" she asked, narrowing her eyes.

"Seeds," I said.

"Seeds? What seeds? Who gave you seeds? Where did you get them?"

I thought it best not to mention where I'd gotten them. "Big Pete Parley doesn't want to marry *you*," I said. It was a mean thing to say and I wanted to say it.

Mama sighed. "It doesn't matter what he wants, Jack. I'm dead anyway." She took the bag of seeds from me, picked some up, squinted at them.

"What is that supposed to mean?" I said, sarcastically.

She went to the window above the sink and stared out into the dark. Under the folds of her evening gown I could see the ruined shape of her old body. "Dead, Jack," she said. "I've been dead for a while now. Maybe you didn't notice."

"No," I said. "I didn't."

"Well, you should have. I went to sleep shortly after your Daddy died and I had a dream. The dream got stronger and stronger as it went on until it was as vivid as real life itself. More vivid. When I woke up I knew that I had died. I also knew that nothing in the world would ever be as real to me as that dream."

I almost asked her what the dream was about but I didn't, out of meanness. In the living room Big Pete Parley was whistling impatiently. The davenport was squeaking under his nervous weight.

"So you see, Jackie," said Mama. "It doesn't matter if I marry Pete Parley or what his motives are in the matter. You are all that counts now. He will ensure your success in the world."

"I don't want to be a success, Mama," I said.

"Well, you have no choice. You cannot gainsay the dead."

She opened the window over the kitchen sink and dumped out the sack of seeds. Then Big Pete Parley came into the kitchen. "Let's go for a walk," he said. "It's too blame hot in this house."

They left by the kitchen door. I watched them walk across the yard and into the dark, unplanted field. Big Pete had his arm around Mama's shoulder. I wondered if he knew, or cared, that he was marrying a dead woman. Light from the half-moon painted their silhouettes for a while. Then the dark field absorbed them.

I went to bed and slept for what might have been days. In my long sleep I had a dream. I was canoeing down a whitewater river that ran sharply uphill. The farther up I got, the rougher the water became. Finally, I had to beach the canoe. I proceeded on foot until I came to a large gray house that had been built in a wilderness forest. The house was empty and quiet. I went in. It was clean and beautifully furnished. Nobody was home. I called out a few times before I understood that silence was a rule. I went from room to room, going deeper and deeper toward some dark interior place. I understood that I was involved in a search. The longer I searched, the more vivid the dream became.

When I woke up I was stiff and weak. Mama wasn't in the house. I made a pot of coffee and took a cup outside. Under the kitchen window there was a patch of green shoots that had not been there before. "You got something for me?" I said.

A week later that patch of green shoots had grown and spread. They were weeds. The worst kind of weeds I had ever seen. Thick, spiny weeds with broad green leaves tough as leather. They rolled away from the house, out across the field, in a viny carpet. Mean, deep-rooted weeds, too mean to uproot by hand. When I tried, I came away with a palm full of cuts.

In another week they were tall as corn. They were fast growers and I could not see where they ended. They covered everything in sight. A smothering blanket of deep green sucked the life out of every other growing thing. They crossed fences, irrigation ditches, and when they reached the trees of a windbreak, they became ropy crawlers that wrapped themselves around trunks and limbs.

When they reached the Parley farm, over which my dead mother now presided, they were attacked by squadrons of helicopters which drenched them in poisons, the best poisons chemical science knew how to brew. But the poisons only seemed to make the weeds grow faster, and after a spraying the new growths were tougher, thornier, and more determined than ever to dominate the land.

Some of the weeds sent up long woody stalks. On top of these stalks were heavy seedpods, fat as melons. The strong stalks pushed the pods high into the air.

The day the pods cracked a heavy wind came up. The wind raised black clouds of seed in grainy spirals that reached the top of the sky, then scattered them, far and wide, across the entire nation.

I'm not the only writer who has used fairy tales as models for stories. Angela Carter, the late English writer, made a career of writing stories of contemporary life couched in the form of fairy tales, myths, and legends. And why not? The ancient folk tales were as full of betrayed innocence, deceit, and murderous brutality as any modern story. Though their moral intent was often obscure, they had roots that reached back to the earliest heart of humanity. The point has been made that all the dynamic structures of the human psyche have been catalogued, in the form of symbols and archetypes, in folk tales. And why shouldn't this be so? Human experience goes back tens of thousands of years. Why wouldn't we have established a foundation of immutable, rock-bottom truths about our nature in the stories we have been telling each other over those aeons? What other purpose could these ancient tales have had?

ASPECTS OF FORM

Of the various aspects of form, the *voice* that tells the story is perhaps the most crucial. "Once upon a time there was an old king who had three sons" is a voice we immediately recognize. But what about this voice?

> So the girl picks a rose; pricks her finger on the thorn; bleeds; screams; falls.
>
> Weeping, the Count got off his horse, unfastened his breeches and thrust his virile member into the dead girl. The Countess reined in her stamping mare and watched him narrowly; he was soon finished.
>
> Then the girl began to melt. Soon there was nothing left of her but a feather a bird might have dropped; a blood-stain, like the trace of a fox's kill on the snow. . . .

This is from Angela Carter's "The Snow Child." Her use of speedy—almost impatient—declaratives marks this fairy tale as contemporary adult fiction. The necrophiliac count could easily be a character in a modern novel. (Cormac McCarthy's novel *Child of God* has a necrophile as its central character.)

Carter retells "Little Red Riding Hood" in a story called "The Werewolf." In it, Grandma and the wolf are one and the same. The girl, after surviving an attack by the wolf in the woods by cutting off the wolf's right forepaw, visits Grandma, only to discover "a bloody stump where her right hand should have been, festering already." The villagers determine that Grandma is a witch after discovering a supernumerary nipple in the form of a wart on the severed hand—a sure sign of witchery. This unnatural nipple allows her familiar to suckle. The villagers then stone Grandma to death. Make what you will of the psychology of these stories, they have, like certain dreams, the power to disturb your day.

Virginia Woolf's "Kew Gardens" was recognized as a major departure in the form of the short story. Published in 1918, this story, even today, seems a bit radical. The narrating voice regards with *equal importance* flowers, insects, snails, and human beings. There are no characters of central importance, no conflicts, no plot, no dramatic diversions, nothing to redeem, nothing to condemn—the human condition and all its attendant drama goes unnoticed. People come and go, their idle chat recorded, and sometimes their thoughts, but nothing develops into anything resembling a conventional story. There is no "story." We are given an impressionistic view of a moment in the gardens, from the insect-thick loam to the topknots of passing matrons. Even the overheard conversations have no more weight than the chirping of birds. Richard Hugo, in his book on the art of poetry, *The Triggering Town*, writes, "The imagination is a cynic. By that I mean that it can accommodate the most disparate elements with no regard for relative values. And it does this by assuming all things have equal value, which is a way of saying nothing has any value, which is cynicism." I don't know if Virginia Woolf regarded her imagination as cynical, but the argument Hugo makes applies to "Kew Gardens." W.H. Auden once said that poets don't take things as seriously as other people. This is another way of saying that the artist who takes a stance on life that is rigorously objective will not value one subject above another.

But Hugo goes on to ask a crucial question: "Doesn't this lead finally to amoral and shallow writing?" And his wonderful answer: "Yes it does, if you are amoral and shallow."

Virginia Woolf was always aware of the revolutionary nature of form. In her essay "Modern Fiction," she says this: "The proper stuff of fiction does not exist; everything is the proper stuff of fiction, every feeling, every thought; every quality of brain and spirit is drawn upon; no perception comes amiss. And if we can imagine the art of fiction come alive and standing in our midst, she would undoubtedly bid us break her and bully her, as well as honour and love her, for so her youth is renewed and her sovereignty assured." This is a manifesto licensing not only an open attitude toward subject matter but the manner in which subject matter is processed into fiction. Form orders experience; the form the writer is drawn to is *the way the writer understands experience.* Understanding experience is what the art of fiction attempts.

The form of one of Tim O'Brien's stories about the Vietnam War, "The Things They Carried," is the inventory. The story is paced by lists of the things infantrymen carry into combat. This inventory, by juxtaposing the very personal horror of warfare with lengthy and detailed lists of the equipment each soldier carried, has the effect of suppressing any inclination on the reader's part to romanticize that war. There is no glory, only the "endless march, village to village" under the heavy load of equipment and terror. The unrelenting itemization of hardware also has the subtle effect of transferring the weight of these daily burdens to the reader. The form is perfectly suited to a war in which battlefield "successes" were released to the public in official inventories: the body counts, the tonnage of high explosives dropped in carpet bombings, the number of men in the field, the number of sorties carried out by fighter-bombers.

Raymond Carver's story "What We Talk About When We Talk About Love" takes the form of an around-the-table conversation between four friends. They tell each other anecdotes about quirky, violently romantic, and even heartbreakingly pure manifestations of love. Just as in Hemingway's "A Clean, Well-Lighted Place," the story has a static motif. And yet there is a subtle tension that underlies the gin-fueled conversation, and a sense of progress that keeps the reader turning pages.

Exercise

Try this: Invent a form of your own. Make up its rules. Rewrite one of your old stories (or your latest idea for a story) in this form.

Example

A few years ago I needed to meet a deadline for a book of stories. The book as it stood was a little thin. I was getting desperate. Out of nowhere an idea struck me. I'd do a send-up of a romance novel in the form of a villanelle. Each paragraph would correspond to a line in a villanelle. A villanelle is a poem composed of nineteen lines, two of which, the first and the third, repeat in a specific pattern. Dylan Thomas' "Do Not Go Gentle Into That Good Night" is a villanelle. Theodore Roethke's "The Waking" is another. Two of the nineteen paragraphs of my story, "Romance: A Prose Villanelle," would have to repeat. The major difficulty would be the ending. The ending of a villanelle is a repetition of lines one and three. I was writing a short story, not a poem. How could I give it a satisfactory ending by repeating the first and third paragraphs? Well, I had to cheat a little. I had to make a few adjustments in wording. But ultimately it worked.

I filled the book by writing a story from the trumped-up point of view of one of Richard Nixon's jailed advisors. I also did a modern version of Hansel and Gretel. I always find this kind of playing around liberating. These stories came quickly and easily. They were like gifts.

There are other—less lofty—aspects of form that are nonetheless important to the well-being of your story. They must be used with total consciousness of their effect.

FLASHBACKS

The flashback is a technique beginning writers seem to regard as the most essential in their limited repertoire. Their stories often begin with a scene—a troubled couple are having an argument in a Paris bistro; two young men, having dropped out of college, are hiking in a wilderness; a father and his alienated son are on their way to the cancer ward to visit Mom. This scene, typically very short, a page or less, yields to a flashback, usually a lengthy narrative of "How Things Came to Be the Way They Are." And more often than not, the writer gets committed to this flashback, often forgetting to return to the opening scene, thereby stranding the characters as well as the reader. This "method" produces a stagnancy of explanatory prose that suffocates the story that's trying to be told. Often there *is* no story, just a situation followed by a case-history explanation. Situation-and-explanation is a good mind-set to avoid. My advice to beginners is make the entire story happen in the story's present time. If the story begins in the simple past tense—"Sheila liked dogs, but her husband Clyde was afraid of them"—stick with it. Don't digress to the past perfect tense of the flashback: "Clyde was afraid of dogs because he had been bitten by a poodle when he was nine. The poodle had belonged to his Aunt Genevieve. Aunt Genevieve had tried to dismiss the incident, but Clyde had not been mollified. That was the year Uncle Roy took Clyde to San Francisco, where Clyde first became interested in the cable cars. He bought a book that covered the history of cable cars. One day Uncle Roy got sick in the hotel where they were staying and Clyde had to find a doctor. . . ."

Many successful stories do this sort of thing, but in each case the present-time story *is* the story; the flashback merely gives the present-time story depth. Even in a story like Margaret Atwood's "Death by Landscape," in which most of the story is given in flashback, the present-time scene from which the flashback was launched is what compels our interest. The flashback—a camping episode that ends in a tragedy for which the central character feels at least partially responsible—provides the basis for the permanent psychological and spiritual malaise of this character. The tragedy has no meaning in itself: Two girls at summer camp go off by themselves to climb a lakeside cliff. One of them mysteriously disappears. Did she fall? No one knows. Her body is never found. But this can't be *the* story. The story belongs to the girl who is left to bear the guilt, mostly self-imposed, of her friend's probable death. What has *meaning* is the gradual withering of the surviving girl's soul. Here is a telling paragraph near the end of the story:

> She can hardly remember, now, having her two boys in the hospital, nursing them as babies; she can hardly remember getting married, or what Rob looked like. Even at the time she never felt she was paying full attention. She was tired a lot, as if she was living not one life but two: her own, and another, shadowy life that hovered around her and would not let itself be realized—the life of what would have happened if Lucy had not stepped sideways, and disappeared from time.

This character has lived in a state of perpetual distraction. She has gone through the motions of living a life, but she, in effect, died with her friend decades ago. It's a powerful story told in a bold way, a way I would caution beginners to avoid.

Avoid *any* technique until you understand how to use it. A flashback not used judiciously will try to dominate—and thus smother—the story you have to tell.

FLASH-FORWARDS

This technique is rarely used, but it can be effective when the story calls for it. Here's an example of a flash-forward from one of my stories, "Horizontal Snow."

The narrator, an engineering student, is hitchhiking from Minnesota to Seattle. He's been picked up by some unusual characters. They stop in a North Dakota cafe called Mud and Sinkers to get out of a fierce blizzard.

> I wanted to be back in West Seattle, in my parents' big house overlooking the Sound. I wanted to be in my upstairs

room, at my desk, watching the ferryboats at night brilliantly spangled with lights. I wanted to listen to the lonesome call of their foghorns while snuggling deeper and deeper into my old bed.

There were some names etched by knifeblade into the table before me. Rena + Yank. Pete + Vicki. Remember Me, Annette. I concentrated on those names and sipped my coffee, willing the night to pass quickly. I would come back to Mud and Sinkers four years later as a Boeing field engineer, after completing my degree at the University of Washington, the snag in my thinking long gone and forgotten. Carline Minsky from the town of Balfour would be with me, and those carved names would still be here among half a dozen more. Carline was pregnant and wanted to get married, but I told her I already was married—even though my wife had left me several months earlier. Carline broke down, but what could I do? I said I'd pay for the abortion. She took the money, but our little romantic episode ended then and there. Maybe she got the abortion and maybe she didn't. I never found out, nor wanted to.

After another paragraph of this, the narration switches back to the present time of the story. What is the effect? My intention was to give the story a future reference point in order to give the present events a darker, and thus a richer, shade of meaning.

FRAMES: THE STORY WITHIN THE STORY

Chekhov wrote some of his best stories using a framing technique. The frame establishes a mood, an atmosphere, and introduces the characters, one of whom will then narrate the core story. Conrad's "Heart of Darkness" employs a framing story. The initial narrator gives way to Marlowe who tells his harrowing story, not giving the floor back to the initial narrator until the final paragraph. The frame in this story works effectively: The sun is going down, the tide is at its peak—nature seems to hold its breath waiting for Marlowe to deliver his tale.

Chekhov's "Gooseberries," "Ariadne," and "About Love" are stories using this device. Raymond Carver, in what I believe was a conscious homage to Chekhov, wrote "What We Talk About When We Talk About Love" using the frame of kitchen table conversation to allow the interior stories to be told. Carver's frame is relatively "thicker" than Conrad's or Chekhov's, and, consequently, the interior stories are allowed proportionately less space. Carver's frame story gains in relative importance because of this, whereas the framing stories of both "Heart of Darkness" and "Gooseberries" merely establish a mood and a circumstance that prepare the reader for the more compelling interior stories.

TRANSITIONS

Transitions have a minor but important role to play in the structure of a story. How do you get the action from here to there in space and in time? Do you use clumsy machinery, such as "Meanwhile, back at the cabin, McNulty was trying to light his camp stove." Or do you just change paragraphs and go straight to McNulty in the cabin? The latter is preferable. It allows you to drop the tired rhetorical devices such as "Meanwhile," "Later that same day," "At that very moment" so that the new paragraph can begin, "In the cabin, McNulty was trying to light the camp stove." If the transition is to signal a major leap through time and/or space, an extra line of "white space" between the paragraphs can be used. With white space, we can return to McNulty by simply writing, "McNulty was trying to light the camp stove." This extra space is a signal to the reader that the story is taking an unusually precipitous leap forward, backward, or sideways. I've sometimes used asterisks and other pictorial devices to indicate a major transition, but I have come to think of these things as makeshift and intrusive. Use them, though, if you must.

The way you use transitions tests your grasp of how time and space affect the shape of your story. Can you conceive of a short story whose time frame is twenty or thirty years? How are transitions

147

used in such a story? John Cheever's "Torch Song" takes place over a long period of time, perhaps as much as fifteen or twenty years. The story itself seems to function as a series of transitions. I've come to think of its form as "A Life in Continual Transition." Most of it is given in narrative summary, the transitions forthrightly managed in lines such as "He saw Joan again, later that summer, when he was having dinner in a Village restaurant"; "Sometime the next winter, Jack moved from the Village to an apartment in the East Thirties"; "That winter Jack met a girl he decided to marry"; "Jack's wife got pregnant early in the fall. . . .'"; "When Jack's son was less than two years old, his wife flew with the baby to Nevada to get a divorce"; "Jack was drafted into the army in the spring of 1942"; and so on. These effortless, and relentlessly insistent, transitions keep the story moving through vast periods of time as well as space. The confidence of the writer is impressive; his control is total. A lesser talent would struggle with the jumps through time and space, would, perhaps, be more inclined to explain them or justify them with the intent of softening them. Not Cheever. He takes you on a ride that ends in a spectacular scene that in itself justifies all the bold steps leading to it. The shape of this story, if it can be described in metaphor, is double sine waves, one the inverse of the other.

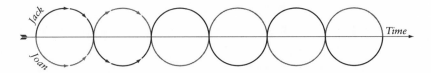

The lives of the two central characters, Jack and Joan, intersect over and over, where the curves meet. The horizontal axis represents the steady progression of time.

"FICTION IS EXPERIMENTATION"

Earlier in this chapter, I applied the term "conventional" to short stories in a way that might suggest to some that most of us writing today are working exhausted ground, and that we had better start looking for new ways to tell stories, ways that reflect changing perspectives on human behavior and the philosophy of phenomena. Nothing could be farther from the truth. Individual stories might need special treatment from time to time, but much of contemporary short story writing remains vital in spite of being "conventional." By conventional, I simply mean stories that represent the reality we in Western civilization have generally agreed upon, even though that reality is constantly besieged by new developments in the cognitive and physical sciences and their subsequent adaptations in the arts.

Some things however aren't susceptible to change: The knife cut on my hand is as real as the cut my grandfather received on his hand ninety years ago. Divorce, though easier to come by, is as emotionally painful now as it was in 1900. Failures in friendship and love are as damaging as they were in Chekhov's time. We still admire courage and are shamed by cowardice. Beauty allures, uglinesss repels, but we still have trouble recognizing either at first glance. Time still moves doggedly in one direction, though its pace varies. And the spectres of sickness and death continue to dog us through our confused and chaotic lives.

Well-drawn fictional characters still persuade us that they live, that their hearts beat and their brains work, that they love and hate or cannot muster enough passion to ignite either emotion. The conflicts look like the conflicts real people endure. And resolution or no resolution, the story is all.

The ingenious metafictions of Jorge Luis Borges, Julio Cortázar, Robert Coover, John Barth, Donald Barthelme, Italo Calvino, and many others play with (and in doing so undermine) the bases of this deeply entrenched tradition, but the conventional method of structuring short stories is still the choice of most writers working today.

Metafiction is a deconstruction of realistic fiction. It can be seen as a corrective that has made readers (and writers) see that many of the unexamined—and thus unconsciously adopted—processes and assumptions of conventional fiction have become somewhat threadbare. Wallace Stevens' remark that "Realism is a corruption of reality" could serve as the motto of metafictionists.

Donald Barthelme's story "Me and Miss Mandible" begins like this:

> Miss Mandible wants to make love to me but she hesitates because I am officially a child; I am, according to the records, according to the gradebook on her desk, according to the card index in the principal's office, eleven years old. There is a misconception here, one that I haven't quite managed to get cleared up yet. I am in fact thirty-five, I've been in the Army, I am six feet one, I have hair in the appropriate places, my voice is a baritone, I know very well what to do with Miss Mandible if she ever makes up her mind.

So the impossible story goes, never budging from the absurd premise that one can be eleven and thirty-five simultaneously. And the absurdities continue to pile up. This is not the way fiction is supposed to work. But Barthelme's story *works*. It delights and fascinates, and we don't care that it abandons the conventions of realistic fiction. We cheer it on.

To certain writers (and Barthelme is certainly one of them), the creative act is not possible if they are confined to forms derived from aesthetic and cognitive notions that have become suspect through overuse and blind acceptance. Just as Cervantes invented the novel by deconstructing the traditional romance with his great parody, *Don Quixote*, metafictionists are engaged in an attack on how we think about story writing, an attack that may result in replacing the old convention with a new convention. It hasn't happened yet, but the state of fiction writing is (as it always has been) in a state of flux and open to revision. That's how any art maintains its vitality and relevance. The recent developments of flash fiction and microfiction—stories that consist of two to five hundred words—can be seen as a deconstruction of the short story's traditional length of two thousand to ten thousand words.

This statement by John Barth gives us a useful way to think about experiments in form:

> We tend to think of experiments as cold exercises in technique. My feeling about technique in art is that it has about

the same value as techniques in lovemaking. That is to say, heartfelt ineptitude has its appeal and so does heartless skill; but what you want is passionate virtuositiy.

The convention we have (and now take for granted) began as bold experiments back at the turn of the century. A story you might read in *The New Yorker* or *The Atlantic* or *Esquire* or *GQ* owes its "conventional" form to the pioneering work of Joyce, Chekhov, Anderson, Woolf, and others. Even the "industrialized" short stories critic Kenneth Allan Robinson railed against in 1924 borrowed their shapes and special effects from the efforts of these earlier artists.

But a story such as Joyce's "Araby" was something very new in the English-speaking world when it was published in 1916. Stephen Crane's fiction was such a departure in technique that some reviewers at the time had trouble understanding the new principles at work in it. H.G. Wells, however, said Crane's work ". . . is the first expression of the opening mind of a new period, or, at least, the early emphatic phase of a new initiative. . . . " Edward Garnett, writing in 1898, said, "The rare thing about Mr. Crane's art is that he keeps closer to the surface than any living writer, and, like the great portrait-painters, to a great extent makes the surface betray the depths." Hemingway immediately comes to mind as the twentieth-century writer who profited most from Crane's groundbreaking approach. Garnett went on to say, "[Crane] is the chief impressionist of our day. . . . If he fails in anything he undertakes, it will be through abandoning the style he has invented."

CONVENTION

Most of my stories are conventional, and I think this is because I am fairly conventional in my view of human nature: Our strengths and frailties have remained constant through the millenia, though our understanding of them has changed as our interpretation of our place in cosmology changed, from central to peripheral or worse. At the same time, every story I write is an experiment, an experiment that forms its own rules. John Cheever, in response to an interviewer's question, said, "Fiction is experimentation. When it ceases to be that, it ceases to be fiction. One never puts down a sentence without the feeling that it has never been put down before in such a way, and that perhaps even the substance of the sentence has never been felt. Every sentence is an innovation."

And yet, most of the stories you have read and will read and most of the stories you will write will look rather conventional. That's okay. It's probably a mistake to try to be original. Originality is something that is part of your nature as a writer or it's not. It can't be acquired. And that's just fine. It's nothing to worry about. The convention is still a strong one, and good writers have made good stories by holding to its precepts.

The terrain the early innovators crossed was hard-won. We honor it every time we put ink to paper. When the convention runs out of gas—as all conventions do—the genius of the moment will give us something new.

8

SPANNING THE CHASM

Stories are made up of narrative, narrative summary, and scenes. These are the fundamental bridge parts—the cables, trusses, and piers—that span the chasm, rim to rim. The chasm is always there: If these connective structures don't hold up, the edifice (your story) goes crashing down.

NARRATIVE

When his hour had struck he stood up and took leave of his desk and of his fellow clerks punctiliously. He emerged from under the feudal arch of the King's Inn, a neat modest figure, and walked swiftly down Henrietta Street. The golden sunset was waning and the air had grown sharp. A horde of grimy children populated the street. They stood or ran in the roadway or crawled up the steps before the gaping doors or squatted like mice upon the thresholds. Little Chandler gave them no thought. He picked his way deftly through all that minute vermin-like life and under the shadow of the gaunt spectral mansions in which the old nobility of Dublin had roystered. No memory of the past touched him, for his mind was full of a present joy.

Narrative is the voice that *tells* the story. Some stories are presented almost entirely in narrative. If the writer relies heavily on narrative, then the voice must be believable and compelling. Otherwise, why should the reader take the narrator at his or her word that what the reader is being told has any truth or relevance in it? For narration always comes across as secondhand information, information once removed from the reader. In the above excerpt from James Joyce's "A Little Cloud," the narrating voice creates no doubt in the reader's mind that it is being faithful to reality. This sense of "truthfulness" is managed by quick declarative sentences and crisp images that stick in the mind. That these sentences are relevant to the story is suggested by the implied characterization of Little Chandler. (He takes leave of his desk and fellow clerks "punctiliously." He is a "neat modest figure." He gives no notice to the hordes of raggedy street children.)

Let's tamper a bit with this paragraph so that what it is saying no longer inspires the reader's confidence.

> Somewhere around quitting time he got up and wandered away from his desk. Outside, under the building's entryway arch, he debated the reasons why he'd left the office before the others. He was a small man, not really old, yet one could not call him young, either. He was a sharp-faced man with little in the way of distinctive features, and yet he was a man who knew what he was and what he was not. He was well liked for that particular quality among other qualities of equal charm, though some thought him hopelessly provincial. He walked with a quick and lively step but with mixed feelings—mostly happy ones, or so he believed—down the street. It was almost dark though the sun hadn't set. It was so cold, so very, very cold. The old houses he walked by cast cheerful, ostentatious shadows. Some street urchins, a common sight in those beleaguered days, drifted by. Some sat on the steps, begging for attention, perhaps love, one couldn't say exactly. In any event, Little Chandler didn't feel it was

his obligation to notice them. He was simply too preoccupied with excited anticipation.

This narrator is so tentative and insecure he has to rely on devices such as bringing in outside sources to vouch for his veracity: "He was well liked . . . some thought him hopelessly provincial." This Little Chandler has no distinctive features, yet is "sharp-faced." So which is it? Or doesn't a sharp face qualify as a distinctive feature? The author has to insert himself into the narrative, thinking the reader will be swayed by his authority: "Some street urchins, *a common sight in those beleaguered days* . . ." The narrator, for want of imagination, has to insist a thing is so rather than offering evidence: "It was so cold, so very, very cold." What are these "mixed" though "mostly happy" feelings? Is the writer not clear in his own mind what his man's motives are? And "cheerful, ostentatious shadows"? Is the writer joking?

What have we lost here? Little Chandler's punctiliousness is gone. His neat, modest figure is gone. The sharp air is gone. The horde of grimy children are gone, as is the wonderful image of them as mice. Specificity is gone—we don't know where we are; it could be London, New York City, or Omaha. And precision is gone: The "spectral mansions" of old Dublin are now anonymous "old houses." "Henrietta Street" has become just "the street." The reader is left to his or her own devices. The reader is left to speculate. Readers do not want to speculate about things that should be crystal clear from the outset. If they are left to speculate very long, they will begin to smirk and then yawn. The bridge falls into the chasm. No bridge, no story. Just debris.

When writing narrative, remember to use clear, declarative sentences. If you want your character to suddenly grow wings and fly, then say so directly, without apology. ("Freddy woke up one morning with great feathered wings growing out of his back." Remember Kafka's "Metamorphosis": "As Gregor Samsa awoke one morning from uneasy dreams he found himself transformed in his bed into a giant insect.") Do not force the reader to grope for explanations. As a poetry teacher of mine once said, "Poetry is presentation, not explanation." I'd say the same thing about short stories.

Have the confidence to *present* without explanation or apology. The reader trusts a confident narrator.

Be specific—identify things by their proper names. A reader wants to be grounded by what is recognizable. Be vivid, be concrete, be aware of the detail that will engrave itself into the reader's mind.

NARRATIVE SUMMARY

> Ignatius Gallaher puffed thoughtfully at his cigar and then, in a calm historian's tone, he proceeded to sketch for his friend some pictures of the corruption which was rife abroad. He summarised the vices of many capitals and seemed inclined to award the palm to Berlin. Some things he could not vouch for (his friends had told him), but of others he had had personal experience. He spared neither rank nor caste. He revealed many of the secrets of religious houses on the Continent and described some of the practices which were fashionable in high society and ended by telling, with details, a story about an English Duchess—a story which he knew to be true. Little Chandler was astonished.

Narrative summary compresses the dramatic parts of a story that would be pointless to present in lengthy scenes. It saves time and space. It keeps the story moving forward but prevents it from becoming too long.

The value of narrative summary can't be overstressed. If Joyce had not used it here, he would have been obliged to bring Gallaher on stage (in a scene) and let him ramble on about his sophisticated grasp of the world. It would have taken up pages and have served no clear purpose. It would have overloaded the story with Gallaher's physical presence. The reader's fascination with Gallaher would degenerate into annoyance and then boredom. Joyce is saving Gallaher for other and more pertinent displays of his boorishness.

Narrative summary, then, is a way of fast-forwarding a story, of getting through minutes, hours, days, sometimes years of necessary story material, material that would take up far too much room if dramatized in scenes.

Look how adroitly Chekhov, in his great story "Peasants," compresses the day-to-day routine of one of his characters with narrative summary.

> For days Klavdia Abramovna would sit indoors, doing nothing. Sometimes, when the weather was fine, she promenaded on Malaya Bronnaya Street or Tverskaya, with head proudly lifted, feeling like a lady of dignity and importance, and only when she stepped into a drugstore to ask in a whisper for an ointment against wrinkles or red hands, did she feel ashamed. In the evening she sat in her room without a light, waiting for a guest. About eleven o'clock—this happened rarely now, perhaps once or twice a week—someone would be heard on the stairs, and then fumbling at the door, looking for the bell. The door would open, there would be mutterings, and a guest would hesitatingly step into the foyer, usually an elderly, fat, bald, homely man, and Klavdia Abramovna would hasten to take him into her room. She adored the right kind of guest. For her no creature ranked higher or was more deserving. To receive the right kind of guest, to treat him considerately, to humor him, to please him, was the need of her soul, her duty, her pride, her happiness. She was unable to refuse a guest, to treat him coldly, even when she prepared for the holy sacrament by prayer and fasting.

Again, what makes this believable is Chekhov's confident, declarative sentences, his use of telling detail, and, ultimately, his humanity—Klavdia Abramovna has our compassion because she has Chekhov's compassion. We don't pity her, neither do we find her laughable. Chekhov could have taken the time to show Klavdia promenading, stopping to shop in drugstores, entertaining guests, but it would have taken tens of pages to do so, and in this rather long story, it would have been a distraction. By compressing all these events into a paragraph, Chekhov achieves what he wants.

SCENE AND DIALOGUE

"Ah well," said Ignatius Gallaher, "here we are in old jog-along Dublin where nothing is known of such things."

"How dull you must find it," said Little Chandler, "after all the other places you've seen!"

"Well," said Ignatius Gallaher, "it's a relaxation to come over here, you know. And, after all, it's the old country, as they say, isn't it? You can't help having a certain feeling for it. That's human nature . . . But tell me something about yourself. Hogan told me you had . . . tasted the joys of connubial bliss. Two years ago, wasn't it?"

Little Chandler blushed and smiled.

"Yes," he said. "I was married last May twelve months."

"I hope it's not too late in the day to offer my best wishes," said Ignatius Gallaher. "I didn't know your address or I'd have done so at the time."

He extended his hand, which Little Chandler took.

"Well Tommy," he said, "I wish you and yours every joy in life, old chap, and tons of money, and may you never die till I shoot you. And that's the wish of a sincere friend, an old friend, you know that?"

"I know that," said Little Chandler.

"Any youngsters?" said Ignatius Gallaher.

Little Chandler blushed again.

"We have one child," he said.

"Son or daughter?"

"A little boy."

Ignatius Gallaher slapped his friend sonorously on the back. "Bravo," he said, "I wouldn't doubt you, Tommy."

Little Chandler smiled and looked confusedly at his glass and bit his lower lip with three childishly white front teeth.

"I hope you'll spend an evening with us," he said, "before you go back. My wife will be delighted to meet you. We can have a little music and—"

"Thanks awfully, old chap," said Ignatius Gallaher,

"I'm sorry we didn't meet earlier. But I must leave tomorrow night."

"Tonight perhaps . . . ?"

"I'm awfully sorry, old man. You see I'm over here with another fellow, clever young chap he is too, and we arranged to go to a little card-party. Only for that . . ."

"O, in that case . . ."

"But who knows?" said Ignatius Gallaher considerately. "Next year I may take a little skip over here now that I've broken the ice. It's only pleasure deferred."

"Very well," said Little Chandler, "the next time you come we must have an evening together. That's agreed now, isn't it?"

"Yes, that's agreed," said Ignatius Gallaher. "Next year if I come, *parole d'honneur.*"

Scenes are the most powerful of the three basic structural elements because they put the characters on stage where we can see them. We hear them talk, watch them move, experience their milieu. When the characters are on stage, they reveal themselves in ways a narrator cannot. If a narrator comments that Little Chandler is modest and shy, or that Ignatius Gallaher is a patronizing bully and blowhard, you might ask irritably (and justifiably) to be shown these qualities. In the above scene, we catch Gallaher red-handed. There can be no doubt who and what he is. Joyce adds to the effect he wants by never calling him anything but "Ignatius Gallaher," the six syllables of his name repeated over and over again, like a formal title. And Gallaher's blarney is mixed with his measured British English: "I'm awfully sorry, old man. You see I'm over here with another fellow, clever young chap he is too, and we arranged to go to a little card-party. Only for that . . ."

This diction, in Gallaher's mind, elevates him above the provincialism of Dubliners like Little Chandler. And the narrator doesn't need to tell us that this is so; he lets Gallaher demonstrate it.

The main feature of the scene is dialogue. And the main objectives of dialogue are to reveal character, to bring relationships into sharp focus, and to advance the story. In the above scene, Gallaher is carefully stripped of all pretense of friendship. He is not Little Chandler's friend, but a self-important braggart who only wants to inflate his image at Little Chandler's expense. He is, in fact, contemptuous of Little Chandler, and the reader can easily imagine him cracking jokes about Little Chandler later that evening at his "card-party."

While dialogue must have all the spontaneity of real-life speech, it is in fact nothing like real-life speech. It is a carefully timed give-and-take: a slow dance, a brisk sparring session, or a merciless pummeling. It is carefully and artfully crafted.

Real-life speech is halting, abbreviated, often distracted, and filled with stunning irrelevancies and wide digressions. It often seems to have no direction. Dialogue is efficient and to the point. Characters, by speaking to each other, blossom on stage; what they say keeps the story moving.

GESTURES

Dialogue can be augmented by gestures. When we speak, we don't sit or stand like wooden carvings. We move our hands, our eyes narrow or widen or the skin around them crinkles, we turn our heads or touch our chins, we bite our lips or we blink back tears. We do a lot of things with our bodies as we speak. The writer of course doesn't need to catalogue all these gestures and twitches, but some should be included to either confirm or gainsay what is being said. A man unable to express his rage might compress his lips and his nostrils might turn white and flare even though he is murmuring obsequious words of gratitude. A woman who does not like children might pat the head of her best friend's child in a stiff-armed manner as if warding off a slobbering dog, all the while making friendly noises to it. I once saw a dignified gray-haired woman in Sprague, Washington, wearing an expensive blue suit, a flowered hat, white gloves, and black heels, elaborately clear her throat and spit voluminously into the street—a gesture that thoroughly undermined the image she wanted the world to see. Such telling gestures reveal an internal truth despite the character's efforts to camouflage it.

In Doris Lessing's story "To Room Nineteen," a story about a disintegrating personality, the principal characters face a critical moment:

> He [Michael] was again lying on his back, his blond head on his hands, his elbows angled up and part-concealing his face. He said: "Then Susan, I have to ask you this question, though you must understand, I'm not putting any sort of pressure on you. . . . Are things going to go on like this?"
>
> "Well," she said, going vague and bright and idiotic again, so as to escape: "Well, I don't see why not."
>
> He was jerking his elbows up and down in annoyance or in pain, and, looking at him, she saw he had got thin, even gaunt; and restless angry movements were not what she remembered of him.

The gestures here amplify the emotional content of what's being said. Michael's gestures are so out of the ordinary that Susan does not recognize them—and, consequently, *him*. This concretizes alienation with choreographed precision. Lessing's use of the abstract adjectives "vague," "bright," and "idiotic" works well in this context, especially when they are followed by the phrase "so as to escape."

Mavis Gallant's "My Heart Is Broken" consists of a conversation between two women, one very young. The young woman is lying on a bed indolently polishing her nails while receiving advice from the older woman. The older woman is in a rocking chair, trying to cull information from the nineteen-year-old woman who claims to have been raped. The story takes place in the Canadian wilderness, in a road-construction camp. The young woman is preparing to leave the camp with her husband. The older woman, Mrs. Thompson, doesn't buy the rape story, believing, rather, that the girl, Jeannie, is promiscuous:

> "I came straight over here, Jeannie, because I thought you might be needing me." Mrs. Thompson waited to hear

she was needed. She stopped rocking and sat with her feet flat and wide apart. She struck her knees with her open palms and cried, "I told you to keep away from the men. I told you it would make trouble, all that being cute and dancing around. . . ."

Mrs. Thompson, by stopping her rocking chair, planting her feet, and slapping her knees, gives weight to the admonishment that follows.

Throughout the story, Jeannie continues to polish her nails, showing no emotion over the alleged rape, which happened not long before Mrs. Thompson's arrival at Jeannie's cabin. The story is full of telling gestures that invest the characters with devastating insensitivities to their own predicaments.

In Hemingway's "Soldier's Home," Krebs, having just returned from the bloody World War I battlefields of Europe, endures his mother's pious lecturing:

> "I've worried about you so much, Harold," his mother went on. "I know the temptations you must have been exposed to. I know how weak men are. I know what your own dear grandfather, my own father, told us about the Civil War and I have prayed for you. I pray for you all day long, Harold."
>
> *Krebs looked at the bacon fat hardening on his plate.*
> (My italics.)

Nothing Krebs could have said reveals his mind better than that simple gesture. Krebs went away a boy and came back home a veteran of the most murderous war ever fought. His mother only sees the boy who went to war, not the man who came back. Her easy moralizing can only be responded to with a gesture.

Dialogue augmented by gestures can identify characters in terms of their social classes, their regional origins, their frames of mind, their attitudes in general. It can create tension, diffuse tension, reveal power differentials. Here's an example:

"What time do you want to go there?" Jake asked.

Yvonne turned from the stove. She took a deep breath. "I'm not going. I *told* you."

"Listen up, you get there early it'll look better for you. Malone, he appreciates that."

"I don't care how it will look. And Malone can take a flying leap into hell with all the rest of that scum."

Jake worked a toothpick between his top front teeth. His eyes went sleepy and distant, as if this thing had been settled some time ago and these last arrangements were routine. "You go now, you'll be back here before seven," he said. "It'll look better you gettin' there early. You shouldn't talk trash about Mr. Malone. You want to take the Ford or you want me to drive you? If I drive it might cost you points with the big boys."

Yvonne began stirring the stew again. "I've got three children to think about. I'm not doing this any more. I'm out."

"All right," Jake said. "I'll drive you. You run and get y'self pretty now. Don't worry none about the kids." He took out his toothpick and examined it closely.

"Oh, please," she said. "Jake, *please.*"

Jake twisted the cap off another beer. He got up and went to the stove and turned it off. He took the wooden stir spoon from Yvonne. "I believe this stew's *cooked,*" he said, lifting the spoon to his lips.

"You bastard," she said, defeated.

"Good stew," he said.

Notice the choreography of gestures in this partial scene: Jake works a toothpick between his teeth. Yvonne takes a deep breath. Jake opens a beer, turns off the stove, takes the stir spoon away from Yvonne, tastes the stew. In its own way, this kind of dance— this body language—acts very much like dialogue. Not much of this is needed; a little goes a long way. But naked dialogue, dialogue that just hangs bodiless in space, can create a disorienting sense of unreality, as in the example:

"What time do you have?" he asked.

"I've lost my watch. I think it's about noon," she said.

"Oh no. I'm late again."

"Didn't they warn you already? One more time and you're out of a job?"

"Not my kind of work anyway."

"A job is a job," she said.

"No, it isn't. A job sometimes is a straight jacket."

"Look, this is the best position you've had in a year."

"That's what Mother says."

"Because it's true. You lose this one, you might as well get on the street with a tin cup."

"You're brutal."

"No, I'm realistic."

"Same thing."

You can get away with this sort of writing for a while *if* you've prepared the reader for it with a description of the setting and a sense of who these characters are. Hemingway does it in "A Clean, Well-Lighted Place," but that story has a static quality that requires a minimal use of gesture. The above scene, however, through a paucity of images and gestures, tends to exclude the reader from the experience. If all the dialogue in the story were handled this way, and if the narrative sections of the story lacked specificity and concreteness, it would be very hard to convince a reader to stick with it.

Exercise

Imagine two people, a man and a woman, sitting in a restaurant. One knows something the other ought to know but is having a hard time bringing himself (herself) to mention it. Before you begin, decide who these two people are and what the difficult piece of knowledge is. Also, picture a restaurant, someplace you've been recently. Let that be your setting. Now write one page of dialogue between these two people in which the bad news is never mentioned explicitly. Use images from the setting to help establish the emotional mood. Allow your characters four or five physical gestures, gestures that have the impact of dialogue.

Example

"What are you going to order, Frank?" Anita said.

Frank squinted at the chalkboard behind the cash register. The special was chicken dumplings. "I don't know. Maybe the dumplings."

It was hot in the restaurant. Slow-turning ceiling fans barely disturbed the air. A fat, blue fly preened itself on the sugar jar. "Why *this* place, Anita?" Frank asked.

Anita shrugged. "It was close and cheap. Besides, I didn't ask you to come here for the cuisine."

"Oh?"

"I needed to see you again."

Frank leaned back in his chair, wiped a trickle of sweat from his forehead. "Is this about your sister? Is she seeing that psychopath again?"

"It isn't about Veronica," she said, her eyes distant. "It's about me."

"Right," Frank said, snapping his napkin at the fly. "I should've known. It's always about you, isn't it?"

I shouldn't have to tell you that the use of "he said" and "she said" is perfectly all right. But some teachers, teachers who were themselves not writers, used to warn against the monotony of the word "said." This was wrong-headed advice. The truth is, "he said"/"she said" is a useful convention that has no visibility. If it has no visibility, it can't be boring or call attention to itself. It simply acts like punctuation, and the purpose of punctuation is to prevent confusion. What is visible, what calls unwarranted attention to itself, is the "imaginative," "nonboring" alternative.

"What's for breakfast?" he intoned.

"Same as usual," she offered.

"I detest eggs," he opined.

"No more than I detest you," she retorted.
"You can't mean that, Bernice!" he expostulated.
"There are times when I really *do*!" she amended.

Here's another, less bizarre, example.

"Where have you *been*?" she demanded.
"I got lost," he explained.

This isn't quite as ridiculous, but even so, the writer doesn't respect the reader's intelligence. It should be clear from the context of the scene that the first line *is* a demand and that saying so is redundant. In the same way, the second line is clearly an explanation. Why would the writer think the reader isn't capable of seeing this on his or her own? Readers don't want or need to be told what a line of dialogue means or what its emotional impact is.

"I'm tired of you and your excuses!" she exclaimed vehemently.

If the reader can't see the exclamation or the vehemence from the context of the scene, then the writer has not done the job.

And this from a best-selling novel (a mysterious suitcase has been retrieved from the ocean; one of the men who finds it thinks it might be full of drug money):

"Let's see what's inside!" he said eagerly.

There are exceptions of course. Sometimes you can actually augment a line of dialogue with a descriptive phrase or adverb. I'm only suggesting that this is usually not necessary. Here's one of the exceptions, taken from "A Little Cloud":

"But who knows?" said Ignatius Gallaher considerately. "Next year I may take a little skip over here now that I've broken the ice. It's only pleasure deferred."

Here the use of the adverb "considerately" brings into sharp focus Gallaher's condescending tone. Without the adverb, the *way* he speaks this line might not be fully perceived.

Another no-no is when the writer uses dialogue to give the reader information that should have been given in the narration, as in the following:

> "Did you have a good day at your job at Durable Garden Tools, honey?" she said.
>
> "I sure did, babe. Since my promotion, I've been killing them at work. I guess I'm super motivated now."
>
> "I'm thrilled, hon. But here's more good news, our adopted children, Babsie and Norman, have been elected to the junior high student council!"

This is worse than amateurish, but even professional writers, though more subtle, sometimes misuse dialogue this way.

DIALECT

Finally, a word about dialect. Unless you know the dialect you want to use very well, don't use it. If you grew up in a region that has its own unique dialect, then you probably have a good grasp of it and will use it with intelligence and respect. But if you're an outsider, your job is infinitely more difficult.

I grew up in southern California, in a white, working-class neighborhood. If we had a dialect, I was too imbedded in it to notice. Some of the kids I grew up with were dustbowl transplants, and they brought the dialects of their regions—whether it was Oklahoma or Arkansas or the Texas panhandle—with them, but they quickly learned to adopt the speaking style of southern California kids—hip, slangy, cool—which we, in turn, learned pretty much from the movies. Shortly after the movie *Rebel Without a Cause* came out, we began speaking like James Dean, the movie's star. "Well then there now," was a phrase Dean repeated. We adopted it, as in, "Well then there now Daddy-o, you want to scarf up some suds then cruise Mission for strange?" (Translation: "Hi. Do you want to drink some beer then drive out to the Mission Beach area and look for girls we don't know?") We were mostly ignorant and inexperienced posers. This oh-so-cool talk made us seem sophisticated, worldly, jaded with experience when we were none of these things.

If you must use dialect, do your research. Don't assume all Southerners speak alike, or that all people of a particular ethnicity use the same inflections and elisions. Remember, people are individuals, and once you try to force a dialect on an individual, you run the risk of turning that character into a stereotype. Nothing will flatten your story faster than a stereotype.

A safe way to present dialect is to suggest it through word selection and syntax, rather than to duplicate it by tampering with spelling. When I see gross misspellings, I become wary—am I getting the language accurately, or is the writer trying to pull a fast one?

But here is some authentic dialect writing, complete with misspellings, from the Richard Wright story "The Man Who Was Almost a Man."

> "Howdy, Dave! Watcha want?"
>
> "How yuh, Mistah Joe? Aw, Ah don wanna buy nothing. Ah just wanted t see ef yuhd lemme look at tha ol catlog erwhile."
>
> "Sure! You wanna see it here?"
>
> "Nawsuh. Ah wans t take it home wid me. Ahll bring it back termorrow when Ah come in from the fiels."

This is about as extreme as dialect writing can get, but this story could not be told in any other idiom. Richard Wright knew this dialect—there are actually *two* dialects here, that of a seventeen-year-old African-American boy and that of an adult white storekeeper—and I take it on faith that the writer got it exactly right.

And here's how Eudora Welty manages dialect in her story "Why I Live at the P.O." without using reconfigured spellings:

> So as soon as she got married and moved away from home the first thing she did was separate! From Mr. Whitaker! This photographer with the popeyes she said she trusted. Came home from one of those towns up in Illinois and to our complete surprise brought this child of two.
>
> Mama said she like to make her drop dead for a second.

"Here you had this marvelous blonde child and never so
much as wrote your mother a word about it," says Mama.
"I'm thoroughly ashamed of you." But she wasn't.

Everything is spelled in normal fashion, but the tone and syntax
of the sentences establish a voice we recognize generally as southern. This voice is clearly not from the Northeastern seaboard; it is
not Midwestern; it is not from the West Coast. Whether the reader
can identify it as Mississippian rather than, say, Alabaman, is another question. Maybe the reader doesn't have to. If Welty has been
true to the dialect of her region—and I know she has been—then I
assume a trained linguist would be able to pinpoint its source.

William Faulkner works both of the techniques used by Wright
and Welty into this piece of dialogue from "Barn Burning":

"Likely hit ain't fitten for hawgs," one of the sisters said.
"Nevertheless, fit it will and you'll hog it and like it,"
his father said.

There are two different voices here, both from the same region,
speaking distinct dialects. You can't do this unless you have an
intimate grasp of the voices you want to represent.

When a story compels me to write dialect, I get very nervous. I
have a good ear, but no matter how good that ear is, it can't get
everything about a dialect right. So I usually make one or two gestures toward it, hoping it comes out sounding all right. Imagine
Henry James trying to write the dialects in *Huckleberry Finn*. Imagine William Faulkner taking on the urban (and urbane) voices in a
Saul Bellow novel. Imagine Truman Capote burrowing (I usually
hate puns) into the heroin nightmares of *Naked Lunch*, or William
Burroughs detoxing his brains to write *Breakfast at Tiffany's*.
Whew! I can't make those imaginative leaps.

All good writers know their fictional as well as their linguistic
territory; they stake it out early and stay within its bounds. Here's
a motto: Write only what you *can* write. It's a silly motto because
that's all any of us does, anyway.

Even so, some people, just starting out, don't seem to grasp this little truism. If they were born and raised in working-class west Texas and have never traveled, they might try to write about people who were born and raised in the Hamptons and who spend their winters on the Amalfi coast. Or vice-versa.

Am I saying, write what you know? Yes, I am. (I'll make adjustments to this opinion later.)

In this chapter I've talked about narrative, narrative summary, and scene as if they were completely distinct elements and as if they are somehow grafted onto each other. This is a mechanistic way of looking at short story writing, and, as such, not totally accurate. Narrative and narrative summary often occur within scenes, and scenes, or miniscenes, can be embedded in patches of narrative or narrative summary. There are no rules governing how or when you are permitted to do this. You use whatever the story demands. Some stories are told solely in narrative, others solely in dialogue. What works, works.

The only criterion is need, and the only requirement is clarity. As Stendhal said, "I see but one rule: to be clear. If I am not clear, all my world crumbles to nothing."

9

POINT OF VIEW

Point of view is the single most deterministic element of form. The stance the narrator takes in regard to the story determines not only how the story will be told but also how the story's ultimate effect will be perceived by the reader. The consciousness through which the events of a story are filtered biases the story in a unique way. When the bias changes, the story changes. As Percy Lubbock stated in his classic work *The Craft of Fiction*—an early study of technique—"The whole intricate question of method, in the craft of fiction, I take to be governed by the question of the point of view—the question of the relation in which the narrator stands to the story."

You have to make a nonbinding decision from the outset, before you commit the first word to paper. Your decision will answer these questions: Whose story is it? Who is going to tell it? You may not know the answers initially. You may have to experiment with a variety of approaches before hitting on the one that triggers your enthusiasm, your intuitive sense of "rightness."

The process might go something like this: You have the bare bones of an idea, the germ of the story. The idea consists of a few characters in a situation. The idea—two couples on vacation, say—appeals to you. One of the men is a burned-out high school teacher, the other an unemployed systems analyst. The systems analyst is an annoying know-it-all. The wives of these men are enjoying the trip uncritically, but the burned-out school teacher feels trapped. He's going to have to spend the next few days being a reluctant audience for the pontificating systems analyst.

At this point, you only have a first scene in mind: The couples are in a sports utility vehicle, somewhere in the Idaho mountains. The know-it-all, driving the SUV, is holding forth on the geological formations of the area.

This isn't much, but you trust your intuitive notion that lurking in the dynamics of this situation lies a good story. You don't know what's going to happen yet, and that's good. You want to be surprised. (No surprise for the writer, no surprise for the reader.) At this point you don't have the first clue as to what's going to happen. You just want to get that first paragraph or two written in a way that makes you feel you've got a lock on the story that's about to reveal itself to you. Your choices for the narrating voice are somewhat daunting.

Here they are:

1. first-person participant
2. first-person peripheral
3. third-person limited omniscience: participant
4. third-person limited omniscience: peripheral
5. third-person full omniscience
6. objective

Since there are four characters in the story, each of the first four choices yields four possibilities. The last two yield only one each. Add them up. *There are eighteen possible points of view.* How do you choose the one that's going to yield the best story?

Before we go further with this, let's define each of these six methods.

FIRST-PERSON PARTICIPANT

The story is being told by a character who calls himself or herself "I." This first-person narrator is involved with the events of the story in such a way that the outcome will affect his or her life directly; that is, this person is *the* central character.

There are countless examples of stories written in this way. John Cheever's "Goodbye, My Brother," Amy Tan's "Rules of the Game," Larry Brown's "Samaritans," James Joyce's "Araby," V.S. Pritchett's "The Diver," and Grace Paley's "Wants" are but a few.

As we discussed in chapter five, this first-person voice shouldn't be confused with the author even when such an identification seems tempting. The narrating "I" is not John Smith the author, but John Smith's puppet. The puppet may resemble John closely, but John knows that—even when the writing is close to autobiographical fact—the very act of composition alters factual reality, by omission if nothing else. To compose an orderly narration that leads to a singular effect, the writer has to choose images and events selectively. This selection, even though based in some reality, produces a fiction. I suppose you could say the same for nonfiction—that, since even a narrative that purports to tell the *truth* can't include every single detail of a given event, from traffic noise to dust motes in the air, it is incapable of re-creating reality. Factual truth is betrayed by the necesssary act of selection.

The chief advantage of this method of writing a story is the confiding nature of the first-person voice. This voice breathes words right off the page. It tells the reader—in an atmosphere intimate as the confessional—about an event of pivotal importance. In competent hands, the spell this voice weaves is powerful. It's hard not to listen. "If the story teller is in the story himself," Percy Lubbock says, "the [teller] is dramatized; his assertions gain in weight for they are backed by the presence of the narrator in the pictured scene."

I personally enjoy composing in first person. However, some writers find it weak. (Henry James had contempt for it. He called it "that accursed autobiographic form which puts a premium on the loose, the improvised, the cheap and the easy.") That's a bit harsh, but the form does have some limitations. The narrator, for example, is as invisible as a ghost. He or she can't be described, except by verbal gymnastics that inevitably call attention to themselves, as in this example:

> I glance at myself in the full-length mirror. Ah, yes—
> there I am, tall and good-looking. I weigh two hundred
> pounds, but it is all hard, well-defined muscle, not the heavy
> slabs of beef you see on powerlifters. No, my body is
> sheathed in sinew meant for speed and endurance. My
> finely spun blond hair shines in the morning light. My blue
> eyes are clear, suggesting a shrewd appraisal of all they see,
> yet there are flashes of mischief in them. My dimpled chin
> accentuates the excellent cut of my jaw. Whenever I enter
> a crowded room, conversations stop and all eyes turn to-
> ward me.

This stomach-turning self-description might work in a comic
story about a hopeless narcissist, but it would be difficult to manage
in a character who didn't have this sort of insufferable ego. But
even when a reasonably modest first-person narrator tries to describe himself or herself, it rings oddly in the ear.

> I checked myself out in the barroom mirror. My long
> brown hair was a little wind-blown. My eyes, normally
> blue, were tinged gray. This is what a cold autumn day does
> to them.

As Percy Lubbock says,

> ... the man or woman who acts as the vessel of sensation
> is always in danger of seeming a light, uncertain weight
> compared with the other people in the [story]—simply be-
> cause the other people are objective images, plainly out-
> lined, while the seer in the midst is precluded from that
> advantage, and must see without being directly seen. He,
> who doubtless ought to bulk in the story more massively
> than anyone, tends to remain the least recognizable of the
> company, and even to dissolve in a kind of impalpable blur.
> By his method (which I am supposing to have been adopted
> in full strictness) the author is of course forbidden to look
> this central figure in the face, to describe and discuss
> him. . . . And very often we see the method becoming an

embarrassment to the author in consequence, and the devices by which he tries to mitigate it, and to secure some reflected sight of the seer, may even be tiresomely obvious.

In addition to this difficulty, a first-person narrator with ordinary human abilities can't inhabit the consciousnesses of the other characters, can't be privy to the activities and conversations of the other characters when they leave the vicinity of the narrator.

Ring Lardner, in his story "Liberty Hall," wasn't willing to abide by these restrictions, and so allowed his narrator to report a conversation that takes place beyond her hearing. This magically overheard conversation is a delightful piece of comedy, and the reader is rewarded by it, but it violates the inherent strictures of the method Lardner had chosen.

So what? you may well ask. So this: When a pro like Ring Lardner does it, the reader either doesn't notice or is quick to forgive the infraction. When a novice does it, it usually sabotages the story.

FIRST-PERSON PERIPHERAL

Again the story is being told by someone who calls himself or herself "I," but in this case the storyteller is *not* the central character. This narrator is a reporter of dramatic events that, on the surface at least, are of more interest than the narrator's place among those events. The outcome of the story may or may not cause a change in this person's life.

An example of this method is Melville's "Bartleby the Scrivener." It can be argued that the narrator of this story is the one most affected by the dramatic events and therefore has first claim on our sympathies, but from a strictly technical standpoint, the narrator's relation to the center of the story, Bartleby, is *peripheral*. Bartleby and his psychopathic inertia comprise the gravitational core and ultimate mystery of the tale. Without Bartleby there is no story.

In the same way, Nick Carraway, the narrating voice of *The Great Gatsby*, orbits the life of Gatsby. The orbit is eccentric enough to allow Carraway's distance from the central characters

The Art & Craft of the Short Story

to vary from engagement to complete disengagement. And while Carraway, like the nameless narrator of "Bartleby," may claim our sympathy, the story is not about *him*.

James Baldwin's "Sonny's Blues" is the story of two brothers: one a teacher of mathematics who leads an orderly, contained—if somewhat constrained—life; the other, Sonny, a heroin-using jazz musician. The unnamed narrator is the conservative brother, who, though he knows Sonny's obsession with his art is self-destructive, comes to realize that his efforts to "reform" Sonny are not only useless but wrongheaded. And yet, the center of the story is Sonny, not the narrator.

Ring Lardner's "Haircut" is narrated by an anonymous barber who tells the story of his town's "lovable" practical joker, one of the most hateful men in literature. At one point the narrator momentarily veers off his subject and into his own story about how much is owed him by freeloaders, but Lardner, as if teasing the narrative technique he's chosen, doesn't permit his dim-witted narrator to go off on this track for more than a line or two. The barber interrupts his own digression and gets right back to the matter at hand.

The narrator in this method is typically unnamed so that the focus of the story stays on the main character. The anonymous "I" yields the stage to the subject of its narration. In Melville's "Bartleby," the method is effective because the balanced, compassionate voice of the narrator is easy for the reader to identify with. We trust this voice, we sympathize with it, and, ultimately, we believe it. In Lardner's "Haircut," the first-person peripheral voice works precisely because the narrator is *un*believable, so unbelievable that we see through his misguided monologue to the nasty truth behind it.

The method Lardner uses in "Haircut" is called the unreliable narrator. When the narrator seems not to understand the implications of what he or she is saying, that narrator becomes "unreliable." Lardner uses an unreliable narrator in several of his stories. A novel that raises this technique to high art is Ford Madox Ford's *The Good Soldier*.

THIRD-PERSON LIMITED OMNISCIENCE: PARTICIPANT

Here the story is told from the point of view of the story's central character but in third person. By limited omniscience, I mean that the narrator can report, godlike, the thoughts and emotional condition of this character but, ungodlike, not of the other characters.

The advantage this method might have over a first-person rendition is that the voice of the narrator is flexible. A first-person narration has to be consistent or the story loses credibility. Vocabulary, peculiarities of expression, the way the narrator perceives his or her world—these must remain constant unless the character suffers personality changes in the course of the tale that justify changes in diction and perception.

The flexibility of third-person limited omniscience allows a careful inconsistency in the voice without ruining the overall effect. How can inconsistency (usually thought of as a fault) be of any value? The inconsistency arises from the condition of two minds having access to the story's events—the mind of the central character and the overseeing mind of the narrator.

Here's an example from a Ralph Ellison story, "King of the Bingo Game." The principal character, a man in desperate straits, is watching a run-of-the-mill action movie.

> Everything was fixed. Now suppose when they showed that girl with her dress torn the girl started taking off the rest of her clothes, and when the guy came in he didn't untie her but kept her there and went to taking off his own clothes? That would be something to see. If a picture could get out of hand like that those guys up there would go nuts. Yeah, there'd be so many folks in here you couldn't find a seat for nine months!

Elsewhere in the story, we find a different voice, the diction elevated.

> The man was making some kind of joke, and he nodded vacantly. So tense had he become that he felt a sudden desire to cry and shook it away. He felt vaguely that his whole

life was determined by the bingo wheel; not only that which would happen now that he was at last before it, but all that had gone before, since his birth, and his mother's birth and the birth of his father. It had always been there, even though he had not been aware of it, handing out the unlucky cards and numbers of his days.

Both of these excerpts are given in third person, but the first sounds very much like first person, whereas the second is clearly given by an overseeing narrator, interpreting for us what the character could not. This is a grand inconsistency that makes the reader experience the suffering of the character firsthand but also allows the reader to rise above and understand the roots and the extent of that suffering.

THIRD-PERSON LIMITED OMNISCIENCE: PERIPHERAL

As in first-person peripheral, this story is narrated from the point of view of a character who is not the prime mover of the story's events nor the direct recipient of their consequences. Somerset Maugham's "Rain" is a good example of this technique. The point of view is given to Dr. Macphail, who occupies a neutral position in the drama. He's a decent, intelligent, mild-mannered man—likable and trustworthy on every count. The story, as seen through Macphail's eyes, deals with characters who appear to be at the opposite poles of the moral universe: Davidson the missionary and Sadie Thompson the prostitute. Davidson is a rigid moralist who is at first disgusted and enraged by Sadie's profligacy, but who quickly comes to see her as a God-sent challenge to his powers as a saver of souls. The war between them leaves Sadie an emotional wreck, but Davidson, vulnerable in ways he never thought possible, succumbs to his own carnal self, a self that had been fiercely suppressed. After he has sex with Sadie, the moral polarities are suddenly reversed. Sadie is a whore, but she has never deceived herself. Davidson is deeply self-deceived.

Macphail is the most plausible point-of-view character for these events. The reader finds it easy to identify with him—he is kind, helpful, genuine. And since the story intends to make a strong point about the dangerous consequences of hypocrisy and suppressed carnality, it requires a point-of-view character the reader perceives as having no personal stake in the theme. A narration that has a stake in a story's theme—especially a story such as "Rain"—would open the story to the criticism that it is mere propaganda. For this reason, the story would have been far less effective if Maugham had made either Sadie or Davidson his point-of-view character. For this story to work, the bias in the narration had to be held close to zero.

One of the advantages of this technique is that it allows the writer to conceal critical events, since the peripheral point-of-view character can't always be with the principal characters. These concealed events, when they are eventually exposed, can have the power to surprise. In "Rain" the hidden events, though telegraphed, still result in a brutal shocker of an ending. Mystery writers often employ this narrative method for this reason.

THIRD-PERSON FULL OMNISCIENCE

This technique is more suited to the novel than it is to the short story. Writers who employ it in short stories have to be very skilled. Here the narrator is free to let the point of view slide, from character to character. Used haphazardly, it leads to confusion, and the question, Who is this story supposed to be about? can't be answered with any confidence. And yet some powerful stories have been written in this panoramic way. "The Short Happy Life of Francis Macomber" is an example. In this story, the point of view not only shifts from character to character but is given on two occasions to a *lion*. The story is so seamless that when the point of view shifts, the reader hardly notices.

This smooth sliding of the point of view is something only an experienced writer can manage. If you attempt it, your reasons should be carefully thought out.

In T. Coraghessan Boyle's story "If the River Was Whiskey," the point of view alternates between two characters: a hopeless alcoholic and his young son. Boyle doesn't try to hide the transitions between the two—each switch is boldly signified by a barrier of asterisks. Though the story is presented as disjointed diptychs, it nonetheless tells us everything we need to know about the situation. There is a third character in Boyle's story—the wife of the alcoholic and mother of the boy—who is arguably as important as the other two, but her point of view is not given. Boyle clearly didn't want to give the story that extra dimension. If it had been given, the story would have been longer and more complex. It might not have been a better story, but it would certainly have been a very different story. A rule of thumb: When everything that needs to be said has been said, the story is finished. The trick of course is knowing when that requirement has been satisfied.

Guy Vanderhaeghe's compelling story "Reunion" shifts the point of view among the three principal characters. The effect allows the reader to see a family on the edge of disintegration from the viewpoint of the three people who must suffer through it. The beauty of this story is that our sympathies are with all three of them—the drunk husband, the beleaguered wife, and their child.

To see graphically how a change in point of view changes the story, check out the classic Akira Kurosawa movie *Rashomon*, from your local video franchise. It will illustrate an interesting point for you: An extreme consequence of changing the point of view is a new understanding of what the story *is*.

Rashomon is a story of rape and murder in medieval Japan. It's told from four very different points of view that bear no resemblance to one another. Truth becomes lost in subjectivity. What a character needs to have happened, in order to salvage his or her dignity, becomes that character's reality. Kurosawa seems to be saying our truths are hopelessly subjective and, in fact, there are no truths at all. We each inhabit a world colored and biased by our own needs and expectations. Only the gods see us for what we are. Human beings have no access to absolute truth.

OBJECTIVE

In *The Craft of Fiction*, Percy Lubbock makes the following statement:

> . . . let us start with the purely dramatic subject, the story that will tell itself in perfect rightness, unaided, to the eye of the reader. This story never deviates from a strictly scenic form; one occasion or episode follows another, with no interruption for any reflective summary of events.

In its purest form, the short story is totally objective. There is no intervening consciousness, no point-of-view restrictions, just scenes composed of dialogue and neutral description. In this case, the only consciousness that filters the events of the story is the reader's. The reader's point of view then is the only point of view. A story such as Hemingway's "The Killers" or Carson McCullers' "The Jockey" is told in this manner. Why is this the purest form? Because there is no mediating consciousness between the events of the story and the reader's perception and interpretation of those events. It is, like a stage play, strictly dramatic. What you see is not only *what* you get but *all* you get.

"Pure," however, shouldn't be confused with "best." This objective way of telling a story has its own severe limitations, limitations that you might find too constricting for the particular story you want to write. What it comes down to is your sense of what is right and what is wrong for the story you want to tell. "The subject," Percy Lubbock says, "dictates the method." Sometimes you know immediately how the story should be narrated. Other times, you need to experiment.

Let's look again at the germ of a story outlined earlier in this chapter. Of the four characters, who is the best choice for narrator? This is going to depend on how the writer views the situation, its possibilities, and its effectiveness. The writer can't know these things in the beginning. But he or she can know what "seems" most promising. The writer might start by giving the four characters names. This is always a good idea since a character's name can give the writer a hint about what that character is like. Let's start by doing just that. Here, then, is our cast of characters:

- Dave Colbert—the burned-out schoolteacher
- Marvin Trane—the systems analyst and know-it-all
- Rhea Colbert—Dave's wife
- Freddi Trane—Marvin's wife

Now let's try some story openings from various points of view.

Rhea Colbert, first-person participant

Dave is nervous, I can see it. It's his stomach again. He gets like this. I didn't start the fight this morning, but he makes me feel as though I had. This trip was your idiot idea, he said. He specializes in assigning blame for all his failures, real and imagined, as if he's the center of a world that finds him lacking. It's inverse narcissism. If the shrinks haven't coined that term, maybe they should.

Marvin Trane, third-person limited omniscience: participant

It was good country, Trane knew. It was the best a man could want. Clean air, good water, a place where a man could test himself. It was going to be a good week living in this rugged, unforgiving country, country that cut you no slack. He knew something about this Precambrian basement rock, these grand forests full of ponderosa, old-growth cedar, yew, and larch. Big cats lived here, cougars. Possibly a grizzly or two—he'd heard they'd been moving south the last few years. And not far from here, the Lolo batholith, and its natural hot springs. Maybe he'd be able to teach the sick-looking schoolteacher sitting next to him in the front seat of the Isuzu how to live in the wilderness as if it was home. Not likely, though. The guy looked like he was going to puke his guts any minute. And that wife of his! Anyone with eyes could tell she was fed up with her milk-toast husband. It would only be a matter of time before she dumped him.

Objective

The mountains rose dark before them. Though it was July, the high crags were still creased with snow. The Isuzu Trooper climbed up the nine-percent grade in second gear. The man driving, Marvin Trane, gripped the wheel in his large, sunburned hands. He whistled tunelessly between clenched teeth. The man next to him, David Colbert, a schoolteacher, leaned back into the headrest and closed his eyes.

"Check out that Precambrian basement rock," Trane said, waving his hand at the sheer cliff walls out of which the narrow road had been carved. "We're driving through a geological museum, Davey. We'll be coming into the Lolo batholith soon."

"You wouldn't be kidding me, would you?" Colbert said, his eyes still closed.

"Don't be a pill, David," Colbert's wife said. She was sitting in the backseat with Trane's wife, Freddi. "Try to get into the spirit of a thing for once."

"Davey's just sore at me," Trane said. "He's mad as hell that we didn't stay another night in Coeur d'Alene. He likes resort hotels and fancy restaurants."

David Colbert rolled down his window and let the cool air roar past his ear. His hands had been trembling and now he clenched them into small, white fists. "I'm not sore at anybody," he said. "I just don't go all mushy inside at the sight of mountains and trees."

"Davey's a tough nut," Trane said. "A real city boy. Have no fear, we'll make a happy camper out of him yet, don't you worry, ladies."

"God, I *hope* so," Rhea Colbert said.

"It's true," Freddi said. "Marv's great in the woods. He knows all about survival. He'll teach David how to bivouac. Marv was an army ranger. We'll have a terrific time."

Dave Colbert rolled up his window. He turned to the women. "I *was* surviving. I was surviving just fine."

"Surviving isn't living," Rhea said.

In writing narrative from the objective point of view, the writer needs to be on guard against loaded language. What if in the above piece I had used "loomed" instead of "rose" in describing the mountains? "Loomed" has overtones that suggest impending peril. The word is loaded with subjective implications, while the neutral verb "rose" is simply descriptive. The narrator, by using a word such as "loom," manipulates the reader and thus steps forward as an intermediary between the action and the reader. An objective narrator needs to avoid this.

The writer has to be constantly aware of the small nuances of words—no matter how the narration is presented—but this awareness is of absolute importance in the case of the objective point of view. The dramatic effect of the story must come wholly from the actions of the characters.

MORE POSSIBILITIES

Since there are fifteen more possibilities, we could go on and on with this experiment with the Colberts and the Tranes. It's unlikely you'll ever have to do that. You will have an affinity for one point-of-view method or the other almost immediately.

The story of the four characters on the road together is from a story of mine called "Wilderness." Here's how I started it, using third-person limited omniscience participant.

> Dave Colbert is sick of hearing about the geology of the northern Rockies, but the man driving the car, Marv Trane, is a relentless know-it-all who never passes up a chance to display his knowledge or to correct Colbert's less encyclopedic grasp of the earth's crust. The wives of the two men are chatting in the back seat of Trane's Isuzu Trooper. It was Colbert's wife, Rhea, who suggested the joint week-long trek to Montana. Trane's wife, Freddi—a small, high-strung woman whose eyelids flutter hysterically when she speaks—had been bitten on the arms by her husband and had found a sympathetic confidante in Rhea. They had met

in Relationship Dynamics, a class taught in a local community college's adult education division. The two men had not met each other until yesterday morning, and Colbert—who has already had his fill of Marv Trane—is gloomy with the realization that there is no way to avoid the six days of misery that lie ahead.

There are two other possible points of view that bear mentioning, but not much more. They are second-person singular, and first-person plural. They are difficult and few writers ever have need to use them. Examples of their successful use are few. Jay McInerney chose a second-person narrator for his novel *Bright Lights, Big City*. The novel is a tour de force, an example of the technique at its finest, but probably not something many writers would want to emulate. The repetitive use of "you" has the effect of forcibly implicating the reader in the story's action, risking the reader's resistance. For example, how would you react to a line such as this? "You grovel in front of your husband's boss, you offer your body to him. He says, 'We'll see. I haven't the time right now.'" Does this make you recoil? Of course it does. However, this might be exactly what the writer wants you to do. If the writer is good enough, you might find yourself implicated in a soul-wrenching experience that leaves you exhausted, brutalized perhaps, yet untouched. Which of course is a goal of fiction. Third-person narratives keep you at a somewhat safe distance from the action. First-person narratives bring you closer. But a second-person narration forces you to be an active participant.

On the other hand, the reader might choose to believe the writer is merely showing off his or her skill by using a difficult or unusual technique. If the reader becomes aware of the writer's technique, the story might be seen as an interesting artifice only. Of course a story *is* an artifice, but the fiction writer's job is to hide the carpentry behind the smooth exterior.

William Faulkner's short story "A Rose for Emily" is told in first-person plural. This is another tour de force that is better to study than emulate. The story is told as if the entire town—like the chorus in a Greek tragedy—is telling it, offering a disengaged commentary on the action. "We" is the name of the narrator. The story is in the first-person peripheral mode, but it is the gossipy voice of the community that tells it.

> "At first we were glad that Miss Emily would have an interest . . ."
>
> "She carried her head high enough—even when we believed that she was fallen."
>
> "When we next saw Miss Emily, she had grown fat and her hair was turning gray."
>
> "So we were not surprised when Homer Barron—the streets had been finished some time since—was gone. We were a little disappointed that there was not a public blowing-off, but we believed he had gone on to prepare for Miss Emily's coming, or to give her a chance to get rid of the cousins."

And so on. It's an intriguing story, told in a way only a master could have managed.

When you understand point of view, you have control of your story. If you don't understand it, the story is likely to wallow. You won't be able to say what your story is about. The reader will give up on it. Here's an extreme example of wallowing. I see variations on it in student work from time to time.

> Morgan left the Weigand building the way he came in. The interview went badly. Why had he lied about his education and employment history? Mr. Weigand knew he'd been lying. He could tell by the way Morgan used technical language inappropriately. Weigand had regarded the man before him and had smiled thinly. What a desperate fool this man was, saying "fluid dynamics" when he meant something else altogether.
>
> Morgan knew he wasn't going to pull it off. Project engineer Morgan Fellows! That was a good one! Morgan looked at his skulking reflection in the polished marble walls of Weigand Public Works and saw a man on his way down. He'd

applied for the job based on three weeks of a correspondence course in hydraulics. The only thing Morgan knew about hydraulics after three weeks of lackadaisical study was that water expands when frozen. His instructor, Lou Billings, back in Pittsburgh, told him that it would only take ten weeks to bring him up to speed as a certified technician.

Billings, sitting in his office in downtown Pittsburgh, wondered if he had overstated the case. Well, maybe a little. But after all, ninety-percent of education is self-education, isn't it? If you want to learn, you *will*. And most of his students did well enough, and he had received few complaints. That's what he was paid for, after all—to keep the customers happy. He looked out at the dark currents of the Monongahela River and wondered what Tess, his wife of thirty years, was making for dinner.

Sheila was waiting for Morgan in the car. She saw instantly how wretched he was, how the interview had been a disaster. It was written all over him. It made her sick to see Morgan all hunched up like that, as if someone had kicked him in the stomach. She knew Aaron Weigand, how he enjoyed putting the screws to someone who had no advantage and never would. Weigand could be sadistic. Sheila loved Morgan, but it was becoming clear to her that Eddy had been right about Morgan all along.

And so on.

We are in very shaky hands here. The writer has no grasp of point of view, and so has no control over the story. The story—if there is one—is fragmented as it passes through several prisms of consciousness. It seems as though it wants to be Morgan's story, but then it shifts to his girlfriend, Sheila, after a momentary visit into the minds of Aaron Weigand and Lou Billings.

All this tomfoolery might have some merit if the writer's purpose is playful. But not many writers have the need to make comedy out of a train wreck.

10

DESCRIPTION AND IMAGERY

I suggested earlier that if you did not have an ear for the language, you should try to acquire one. That may not be possible: Some people are born tone-deaf. On the other hand, if you are accustomed to seeing things in a general way rather than in a detailed way, you may be able retrain and discipline your eye.

I must admit that I am deficient in the area of visual imagination. I don't know why this is so—maybe it's something like tone deafness. I realized this early on. Whenever I tried to write a description, something in me would sabotage my will. Reluctance, like a dense fog, wrapped me in its flannel.

I hated it. But did I have to live with it? No. Once you realize you have a weakness, you attack it. You work on it. You read writers who seem to have a great facility in the area of your great failure. I'm not alone in this. Look for vivid images in the stories of J.D. Salinger. You won't find many. What few there are, however, are serviceable, if not brilliant. No matter, his stories are wonderful just the same.

Robert Penn Warren, on the other hand, wrote descriptions that etch themselves into your brain. This is from his story "The Patented Gate and the Mean Hamburger":

> His long wrist bones hang out from the sleeves of [his]
> coat, the tendons showing along the bone like the dry twist

of grapevine still corded on the stove-length of a hickory sapling you would find in his wood box. . . . The big hands, with the knotted, cracked joints and the square, horn-thick nails, hang loose off the wrist bone like clumsy, home-made tools. . . .

Cormac McCarthy has one of the keenest visual imaginations among contemporary writers. Here's a sample from his novel *Blood Meridian*:

It had rained in the day and the windowlights of the low mud houses were reflected in pools along the flooded road out of which great dripping swine rose moaning before the advancing horses like oafish demons routed from a fen.

And this is from "A Wrestler With Sharks," by Richard Yates:

He was . . . a very small, tense man with black hair that seemed to explode from his skull and a humorless thin-lipped face that was blotched with the scars of acne. His eyebrows were always in motion when he talked, and his eyes, not so much piercing as anxious to pierce, never left the eyes of his listener.

"Not so much piercing as anxious to pierce" is priceless. This phrase opens and exposes the man's character with surgical precision. In that perfect instant, we see all of him that we need or want to see.

I learn from such writers. Yet, in spite of their fine lessons, I feel the old inertia settling in when I try to construct a clear picture with words. I have to fight my way through it and hammer out the image. I feel my brain cells fusing with the effort. I stare into space; I begin to nod.

To me, there is something of the conjurer's art in image making. Where there was nothing before, a three-dimensional picture rises, a picture that fixes itself in the mind of the reader as indelibly as if it had been witnessed in real life. How can you forget those dripping swine rising out of pools of light like oafish demons from a fen? I can't. I don't want to.

So, I worked on my weakness. I got good advice from a writer friend of mine. He said it's good to identify your weaknesses because they can become assets. He meant that if you can be objective enough about your own work, so objective that you can spot its shortcomings, then you can focus on those shortcomings—actually converting what was a deficiency into a strength. For this reason, among others, you need to be your own best critic.

The weak muscle got stronger. I still struggle, still feel the fog of reluctance coming on, but I can now make the invisible visible enough to stand and stay and not shimmer and disappear. I feel *rewarded* when I find an image I like. I feel as though I've won something. These images from "The Smile of a Turtle" made me feel like a kid whose box of Cracker Jack had extra prizes in it: "The ionized air lays a charge on the surface of his skin, the hair of his arms stands up stiff and surly, as if muscled, and his brain feels tacked into its casing."

Why is this so important? Remember what Joseph Conrad said: "My task is by power of the written word to make you hear, to make you feel—it is, before all, to make you see." The writer's job is to create a world, whether it's a bedroom or a battlefield, that the reader can inhabit instantly. There is only one way to accomplish this, and that's to represent that world in unique concrete images.

How is this done? Well, the first thing you need to flush out of your brain are the stock images and expressions that, through overuse, have become threadbare. Writers still use them because they are readily available, and if the writer is in a hurry, the temptation to plug one of them into a sentence is strong. Example: "Larson went to a dingy little waterfront bar." How many times have writers described waterfront bars as dingy and little? A thousand? Half a million? Enough times to make it threadbare. Think of all the others:

- Phil was a ruggedly handsome man with an attractively chiseled jawline.
- The towering waves broke thunderously on the beach.
- The palm trees swayed in the breeze under a leaden sky.
- Luis trembled with rage.
- Joan's house was perched high on a cliff.

- Kyle was drawn irresistibly to danger.
- The crimson sun sank slowly in the west.
- Vern stared into the distance, lost in thought.
- Isabel smiled warmly then fear contorted her face.
- Robert slumped down in his chair as hailstones big as golf balls drummed the roof.
- Heinrich's eyes were steely, but Greta's eyes twinkled with delight.
- Loren Asquith froze like a deer caught in the headlights.

These, and thousands more, are stock images. Some are obvious clichés; others haven't quite reached that status yet but are working hard toward it. In any case, they are substitutes for the work the imagination must do. (Remember, the root of "imagination" is "image.") When you don't feel like doing the work of seeing something with fresh eyes, you reach into the grab bag of stock images.

Why is it necessary to see something with fresh eyes? Why can't a stock image do the job? After all, isn't the *story* the main thing, not the assemblage of images that go into it? Good questions. Stock images, after all, are *codes* that both reader and writer share. No decoding necessary. If the writer says, "He watched the train clatter across the trestle," the reader knows instantly what this means. The words automatically and instantly call up the many trains the reader has seen crossing trestles. You've seen one train crossing a trestle, you've seen them all. But what if the writer had written, "He watched the rocking freight cars one by one notch the sky as the train creaked over the trestle." This is something quite different, and—the writer's purpose aside—much more vivid. I can see the notching of the sky by the rocking freight cars; I can even *hear* them. The stock image is just another train crossing another trestle. In the second image, the reader has to do a little work. Not much work, but he or she must make an *imaginative effort* in order to grasp the image. The reader has to cope with the word "notch," has to make the connection between the rectangular shape of boxcars and the idea of them notching the sky. This takes only half a second, but it involves the reader in the creative effort. I think most discriminating readers delight in that. The first image takes no time at all; it asks the reader to remain passive. The first image is more efficient, but the second image makes the story vivid. This should be your motto: If an image is universally familiar, make the reader see it as if for the first time; make it new. It's the sort of thing that makes writing fun—for both writer and reader.

Listen to Chekhov on this subject: "I think descriptions of nature should be very short and always *a propos*. Commonplaces like 'The setting sun, sinking into the waves of the darkening sea, cast its purple gold rays, etc.' [Or] 'Swallows, flitting over the surface of the water, twittered gaily'—*Eliminate such commonplaces*. You have to choose small details in describing nature, grouping them in such a way that if you close your eyes after reading it you can picture the whole thing. For example, you'll get a picture of a moonlit night if you write that on the dam of the mill a piece of broken bottle flashed like a bright star and the black shadow of a dog or a wolf rolled by like a ball, etc."

The stock image—the commonplace image—won't do. Chekhov wants to apprehend the world in the quick indelible way of poetry.

TO METAPHOR OR NOT TO METAPHOR

Metaphors and similes compare things that are essentially unalike. Metaphors insinuate the relationship: ". . . the warm safe island of my bed" (Dylan Thomas). Similes express it directly: "My love is like a red, red rose" (Robert Burns).

Aristotle said analogy is "the greatest thing by far" in the poet's repertoire. In capable hands, simile and metaphor can be useful descriptive tools. In the hands of genius, they can electrify. Cormac McCarthy's simile comparing the dripping swine to oafish demons electrifies the reader; it illuminates the landscape and augments the mood of *Blood Meridian*.

The denizens of hell, delivered to us regularly by horror movies, are always overwhelmingly terrible. Slime is the current major cliché of cinematic horror. All the hideous creatures ooze or drip long glistening strings of gelatinous slime. But nothing in all the horror movies I've seen compares to McCarthy's dripping swine.

Maybe I'm logocentric. No maybes about it. I am. Ah, but then you are too if you've gotten this far with me, and so you must also prefer McCarthy's swine to Hollywood's slime. Good. Stick with our great writers.

Metaphors and similes, however, can be as dangerous as pipe bombs. They can blow up in your face. A student of mine once nearly killed me with his similes. How can a simile kill? Well, if you're a teacher, and if you are essentially a diplomatic person, and if a student turns in a story with similes and metaphors that are so *beyond* far-fetched you feel your sanity being unhinged rivet by rivet, then you almost die struggling to hold your face straight.

Actually, he was a fairly good writer. He was working on a novella, a love story, and it was a good one. No clichéd situations, the characters were well drawn, the action believable, the consequences of the action surprising yet inevitable, and so on. But when he decided to add a spritz of poetry to his prose, it all unraveled. "Her pale eyes glowed like diamond golf balls," he wrote, attempting to impart to the reader the notion that the woman in his story had become sexually aroused. Later, to express a state of shock, he wrote, ". . . Lydia's jaw dropped like a collapsing draw bridge." But the capper was this one: "She rose slowly from the sofa, like a tired but still capable penis attempting erection." Yikes.

You see how lethal this can be? My jaws were clenched like bear traps trying to hold back hysterical laughter. I repeat: He was a fairly good writer. His story was plausible and often effective. But he could not write similes. He could not see the absurdity of the ones he'd made. He had no sense of aptness. My advice to him was simple: Don't try to write them. Don't wreck your story with goofy tropes. Be content to write direct descriptions. Leave the figures of speech to the poets.

Here's a test you might conduct: If a half-dozen capable readers (these *can* be your friends, but if you're in a workshop, you might be better off to trust your squinty-eyed workshop mates instead) regard your metaphors and similes without convulsing with cruel laughter or retching with disgust, then they are probably all right.

Figures of speech have to be taken first on the literal level. For example: "His neck was like a tree stump cut close to the ground." If I visualize a low-cut tree stump, I can easily make the connection between it and a short, massive neck, and the immense strength of the man who has such a neck. This is a bit cartoonish, but it works well enough. But if I ignore the literal level and get fancy, I could be inviting disaster: "His neck was wide and hard as a short stack of dinner plates." Now, when I picture a short stack of dinner plates, I see not only a *thick* neck but also a brittle one, one that is put together curiously, in thin laminations. Whatever the writer is trying to say about this neck is ruined by the simile that *cannot* be taken on a literal level. If the writer's intention is comedic, then such an outlandish trope might be fitting.

If you want to use figures of speech in a comic way, then you are restricted only by the inventiveness of your zany imagination. Richard Brautigan was a master of comic metaphor and simile. Here's one of his from a story about growing up during World War II, called "The Ghost Children of Tacoma": ". . . Mount Rainier towered up like a cold white general. . . . " In a serious story about grown-ups facing a crisis, this sort of simile would wreck the mood. In Brautigan's story, it is charming and appropriate.

Hemingway, our original minimalist, used figurative language sparingly, preferring direct description. In a letter to Bernard Berenson he wrote: " . . . similes . . . are like defective ammunition, the lowest thing I can think of. . . ."

Why? Well, maybe he thought that extensive use of metaphor and simile would fog the crystal clarity of his prose. Maybe he thought simile and metaphor did not give you the thing itself but a substitute thing, and was therefore a distraction. This, from *Death in the Afternoon*, suggests he saw figurative language as a kind of fussiness: "Prose is architecture, not interior decoration, and the Baroque is over." But he could write metaphorically when he wanted to. In *A Moveable Feast*, he gave this estimate of Fitzgerald: "His talent was as natural as the pattern that was made by the dust on a butterfly's wings. At one time he understood it no more than the butterfly did and he did not know when it was brushed or marred. Later he became conscious of his damaged wings and of their construction and he learned to think and could not fly any more because the love of flight was gone and he could only remember when it had been effortless."

This has an elegiac spirit, a poem of praise as well as a lament. Fitzgerald's talent is compared to the natural patterns on butterfly wings, then to the wings themselves, and finally to flight. This triptych analogy is wonderful. But you won't find much of this sort of thing in Hemingway's short stories.

Embedded Metaphor

There is another kind of metaphor that deserves mentioning: embedded metaphors. These are subtle and often go unnoticed *as* metaphor. They are created when an adjective or adverb has connotations that bring other, sometimes alien, qualities to the noun or verb being modified. Here are two from Faulkner's "A Rose for Emily":

> Miss Emily's house was left, lifting its *stubborn* and *coquettish* decay above the cotton wagons and the gasoline pumps. (My italics.)

"Stubborn" is a word we usually reserve for things that have will—people, horses, mules, dogs, and so on. Sometimes a rusty nail "stubbornly" refuses to be pulled out of old siding. Maybe this is a hangover from a time when societies were animistic, when it was perfectly normal to assign *will* to objects. Now that we don't (in realistic fiction, at least) assign will to inanimate things, such words act as metaphors.

"Coquettish" is an adjective pretty much restricted in its everyday use to human beings, usually women. But here, the old house of Miss Emily's (or rather, its decay) possesses that quality. It is a delightful comparison, but uncommon, even exotic.

Exercise

Just to get the feel of the strengths and weaknesses of figurative language (or your strengths and weaknesses in creating it), write a paragraph of description overloaded with similes, metaphors, and embedded metaphors. Push yourself to make startling leaps. Don't worry if some of them seem absurd. You're not going to be asked to show them to anyone.

Example

> Wind speared through the stand of leafless poplars, kicking up rooster tails of the light, granular snow. Ice crystals studded the enameled blue sky like shiny nailheads. Becky pulled her collar up and stamped the gnawing cold out of her shoes—summer shoes, the wrong shoes for this hostile season. Ten days earlier she had been in the green heat of the Bahamas with Nick, warm but miserable, counting the days when she could return to Minnesota. Now she was lost deep in the labyrinth of the north woods. It was early afternoon but soon an unforgiving darkness would shroud the forest and then she would not be able to find her way back to the cabin and its friendly warmth. She was glad to be free of Nick—Nick, who had controlled their lives like an overzealous camp counselor—but now she wished he and his survival skills could be here to build the shelter she was going to need in the next few hours when the cold, which was only stinging now, would become murderous.

This piece is packed with figurative language. Some instances are less evocative than others. "Wind speared through the stand of leafless poplars, kicking up rooster tails of the light, granular snow." This isn't so terrible, but there's a fundamental mistake in it. If you are going to suggest that the wind is like a spear, that's one thing. But if you then go on, in the same sentence, to allow that same wind to kick up rooster tails of snow, then you've shifted the primary image to something else. Spears pass through heavy clothing and the flesh and bones it protects. It's a common image for icy wind. But when it kicks up rooster tails of snow, it acts like a foot or a paw rather than a spear. The writer here has given the reader two images to process, each different from the other. This is a distraction the reader doesn't need.

And what about those ice crystals studding the sky "like shiny nailheads"? Isn't there something jarring about juxtaposing crystals with nailheads? I think there is. Nailheads are flat and meant for hammering. You can't hammer a crystal. I wouldn't use this image. Maybe the ice crystals should stud the sky "like spilled diamonds." I like that better. But then I'd have to worry about the connotations of diamonds—the wealth they suggest, the sort of people one associates with them, and so on.

Then there's the north woods becoming a "labyrinth." Maybe this is okay, but it makes me nervous. The word "labyrinth" forces me to think of Greek mythology *first*—complete with Minotaurs and lost heroes—not the north woods of Minnesota. "Maze," a synonym, might be a better word than "labyrinth." In any case, it's an idea I'd have to struggle with. Then there's Nick, who's controlled their lives like an "overzealous camp counselor." This might be exactly right, depending on the writer's idea of Nick, and the nature of the relationship between him and Becky. "Camp counselor" isn't very sexy. And that's fine, if the relationship between Nick and Becky is short on sensuality, long on hiking, trail mix, and long talks by the campfire.

Is this extreme nitpicking? Spear, foot, nailhead, labyrinth—who cares? I care. And you should care. The short story, like the poem, can't afford even the mildest of false moves.

Here's Flannery O'Connor working this territory in "Parker's Back":

> She was plain, plain. The skin on her face was thin and drawn as tight as the skin of an onion and her eyes were gray and sharp like the points of two icepicks.

I find that kind of writing delicious. I guess I'm addicted to metaphor and simile. I don't think they give you the object secondhand, nor do I think they are mere baroque decoration. Our everyday language is heavily laced with metaphor. We can hardly speak without employing metaphors so deeply embedded we've come to think of them as plain everyday words that have simple denotations.

We have little choice in the matter—the language is packed with metaphor. How could it be otherwise? How do you describe something new without comparing it to something old? When the first chairs were made thousands of years ago, they could only be described in terms of "legs" and "arms" and "backs." There were no other descriptive words available that did the job as well as these.

Airplanes have tails, noses, cabins, and cockpits. Ships have hulls—derived from the Middle English "hulle" which meant "husk"—and some ships still have crow's nests.

Trees have limbs. Rivers and banks have branches. Cars have trunks (or, in England, boots). Books have spines and leaves and jackets. TV sets have rabbit ears. Doorbells and calculators and elevators have buttons. Shoes have toes, heels, and tongues. Needles, hurricanes, and potatoes have eyes. Hammers have claws, saws have teeth, and computers have ports.

Many abstract nouns have their roots in metaphor. "Transgression" once meant "to cross a line." The literal/metaphorical meaning of "excoriate"—to denounce strongly—is "to peel off the skin."

These lists are very long and they'll grow longer as the need to find names for the objects of our experience increases.

SETTING: WRITING WHAT YOU KNOW

"She had a three-bedroom house on Forty-second Street, and from her gabled upstairs window she could see the Brooklyn Bridge and the dark rain forest beyond," wrote a student of mine who had never been east of the Pecos.

Young writers like to write about exotic places (any places that aren't their hometowns are exotic) and often make the mistake of reinventing familiar territory, such as Manhattan, San Francisco, or the dunes of the Sahara.

Here are two rules you should probably adopt:

1. Write what you know.

2. If you feel compelled to write about something you don't know, research the subject so thoroughly that you can appropriate and "own" what you need.

It's always possible to find the special information that will make your descriptions and the dialogue and actions of your characters plausible if not completely convincing to someone who has experienced firsthand what you are inventing from research. What you know is not a fixed quantity. What you know is what you can absorb at any given time or place.

Even so, a writer should probably stick with the familiar. I wouldn't dare write a story about combat in Vietnam. I wasn't there. And even if I went there now as a tourist, to pick up the feel of the place—the colors, the smells, the sights, the feel of the monsoon humidity on my skin—I still wouldn't be able to convince myself that I'd gotten it right.

And yet Stephen Crane wrote *The Red Badge of Courage*, detailing a young infantryman's combat experiences during the Civil War, having only researched the war by visiting the battlefield at Fredericksburg, Virginia, nearly thirty years after the war had ended, and by reading sections of the voluminous *Battles and Leaders of the Civil War*. The battle described by Crane actually took place at Chancellorsville, but did anyone complain? Maybe some veterans took exception. But the general public did not. They felt the novel had the genuine feel of what Civil War combat must have been like from a foot soldier's frontline perspective.

The great writers can make stunning imaginative leaps. Tolstoy could not have witnessed Napoleon's attempted conquest of Russia, yet he wrote of it as if he had intimate firsthand knowledge. He did, however, have experience with armed conflict, having served in the Russian army during the Crimean War. He knew what it was like to be in harm's way.

On the other hand, an inexperienced writer, by not having the language skills to describe what he or she has seen firsthand, can make real-life experiences seem inauthentic. I've seen this happen over and over in student work. After I've criticized a piece for its lack of "authenticity," the student often argues, "But that's what really happened! I was there!" My response to this is, "Maybe that's the problem." The possession of specialized knowledge sometimes deceives a writer into thinking that whatever he or she puts down on paper is, as a consequence of that knowledge, inarguably authentic. But possessing special knowledge is no guarantee that you can represent it well enough in language that it comes alive for the reader. Here's the sad truth: *Poor writing can falsify experience.*

But the question remains: Are *you* going to be able to write about things you don't have firsthand knowledge of? I think it's going to depend on the subject you choose. If you do the research, and if you write well enough, you can probably pull it off.

I'm still not sure I pulled it off in a story I wrote from the point of view of a brain surgeon. I had plenty of firsthand research to guide me—including a copy of my doctor's operating notes—but I still have a flicker of doubt about my accuracy. The story was published in a nationally distributed magazine, and I have yet to receive a letter from a nonplussed neurosurgeon scolding me for getting some technical detail wrong.

Once, in a published story, I made a Farmall tractor *green*. I received plenty of complaints about that blunder. John Deere tractors are the green ones; Farmall tractors are red. That one mistake might have ruined the story for those who are knowledgeable (and oh so sensitive) about the proper colors of tractors.

Be bold enough to take on what you think you can take on. I guess that's my rule of thumb. But I wouldn't write from the point of view of an airline pilot until I'd done some time in the flight deck of a big plane, listening to the pilots chat, learning what the instruments are and how they work, and so on. Would an airline let me do that? Probably not. I'd have to have an "in" of some kind. Unless I was obsessed by my subject, as well as a trifle mad, I'd stop short of getting a commercial, multiengine pilot's certification. But whatever the depth and intensity of my research I wouldn't be satisfied until a seasoned pilot read my story with an eye for errors, large and small, and gave me a passing grade.

Writers of detective fiction often spend time with cops, going on ride-alongs, attending daily lineup, going to a firing range and taking target practice with whatever side arm the police are now using. If you don't do this sort of hands-on research, you risk having your work lack the "texture" of the world you are daring to represent. The reader will quickly detect a counterfeit world.

Exercise

Go to some work environment you know little about—a bakery, a gas station, a funeral home, a bank, a restaurant, a cannery, a nursing home, a shipyard, and so on. Tell the people in charge that you are a writer and that you'd like to do a piece on their establishment. (This won't be a lie—this describes your assignment exactly.) Ask for a tour of the facilities. Ask to interview some workers during their lunch break. Ask if you can hang out for a few days, making notes. (You might be surprised to find that people *like* to talk to writers about what they do.) When you feel you've got a good grasp of the place and what people do there, write a few pages from the point of view of one of the employees. Take the finished pages back to the research site and show it to the person your point-of-view character is based on. If he or she says, "You got it right!" you get an A. Anything less than that is a flunk.

TONE AND ATMOSPHERE

Descriptions of place can set the tone of a story. The tone can be ominous, lighthearted, sentimental, or neutral.

In an objectively written story, description must remain neutral in tone. Carson McCullers' "The Jockey" begins this way:

> The jockey came to the doorway of the dining room, then after a moment stepped to one side and stood motionless, with his back to the wall. The room was crowded, as this was the third day of the season and all the hotels in the town were full. In the dining room bouquets of August

roses scattered their petals on the white table linen and from
the adjoining bar came a warm, drunken wash of voices.

This is an objective rendering of the scene. The "drunken wash
of voices" might seem like a loaded phrase, but it isn't significant
to the story: Its function is only to describe. The paragraph offers
atmosphere (the milieu) but not tone (a subjective bias given to the
milieu).

Compare the McCullers piece to this from Alistair MacLeod's
"The Lost Salt Gift of Blood":

Now in the early evening the sun is flashing everything in
gold. It bathes the blunt grey rocks that look yearningly out
toward Europe and it touches upon the stunted spruce and
the low-lying lichens and the delicate hardy ferns and ganglia-
rooted moss and the tiny tough rock cranberries. The grey
and slanting rain squalls have swept in from the sea and then
departed with all the suddenness of surprise marauders.

There's no careful holding back of subjective bias here. The
words rush out and thrust the reader immediately into the weighted
atmosphere of place. They set the mood for the story that follows.
The rocks yearn, the squalls come in like marauders. The ferns are
delicate yet hardy and the moss has ganglia-like roots. From this
beginning, we expect the story to produce characters who are much
like this natural setting, hardy yet vulnerable, tough and rooted to
place. And later, writing of the houses, MacLeod continues,

Frame and flat-roofed, they cling to the rocks looking
down into the harbour. In storms their windows are
splashed by the sea but now their bright colors are buoy-
antly brave in the shadows of the descending dusk.

If stories can have opposites, "The Lost Salt Gift of Blood" is
directly opposite to the typical J.D. Salinger story. It is almost *all*
description; the poetry of place rings out in melancholy rhythms—
sweet and desperately sad. The poetry of the story is palpable in

every line: "We are warm within the dark and still within the wind. A clock strikes regularly the strokes of ten."

The rich descriptive language contains a story, a sad story that matches the images and tone, but the story is almost incidental—any sad tale could have been held in the poetry of MacLeod's prose. This is a mood piece that induces a gentle heartbreak, even in those readers who come to the story as disinterested outsiders.

Exercise

Write a descriptive paragraph in which you establish a strong tone. Then write the paragraph again, this time changing the tone so that the bias of the atmosphere is completely different.

Example

1.

A river wide as a freeway divided the town into uneven halves. On the north side the houses were small and steep-roofed and set close as teeth and the front yards were narrow brown patches disdained even by weeds. The men here sat on their porches in accustomed indolence. South of the river, there were spacious green parks and wide, airy houses that rested comfortably on half-acre lots. The shouts of happy children rang through the streets and the grown-ups tended their gardens.

2.

The dark river split the town in half. On the north side small houses huddled together in close neighborhoods. Men and women sat on their porches, gossiping or playing cribbage or pinochle. On these warm summer evenings, someone would take up his guitar or harmonica and strike up a toe-tapper. South of the river, large, ranch-style houses were surrounded by manicured lawns and privacy hedges. Quiet, geometrical parks separated the neighborhoods. The people who lived here stayed inside in their air-conditioned rooms during the summer heat.

What can you learn from this sort of exercise? This: Words have weight. You need to weigh your words as if you were writing poems. In a way, you are.

LANGUAGE AND STYLE

A brief word about our language. First of all, it's not your box of convenient tools. If anything, you are its tool. Understand that it must be respected and cared for. *It's all you have.* Word by word, sentence by sentence, paragraph by paragraph, it's the bones and flesh and blood and internal organs of your story. The short story is closer in spirit to the poem than it is to the novel. You can waste words in a novel and the novel will survive. You can never waste words in a poem or short story. Every word has to contribute to the final effect.

Ernest Hemingway respects the language by using it sparingly, cautiously, and with the understanding that if it is used recklessly it can turn on you and ruin whatever you set your hand to.

This is from "A Clean, Well-Lighted Place":

> It was late and every one had left the café except an old man who sat in the shadow the leaves of the tree made against the electric light. In the day time the street was dusty, but at night the dew settled the dust and the old man liked to sit late because he was deaf and now at night it was quiet and he felt the difference. The two waiters inside the café knew that the old man was a little drunk, and while he was a good client they knew that if he became too drunk he would leave without paying, so they kept watch on him.

This is the heart and soul of simplicity and directness. Hemingway does not use the language loosely nor does he seem intoxicated by it. He believes that simplicity cannot hide ignorance or pretended intelligence. Plain language leaves the intelligence exposed. The transparency of his prose is not just something he carried over from his newspaper experience. It is a consequence of taste, of art. This language is dignified and correct and cannot, by its nature, ring false.

Hemingway, in a letter to his editor, Max Perkins: "My temptation is always to write too much. I keep it under control so as not to have to cut out crap and re-write. Guys who think they are geniuses because they have never learned to say no to a typewriter are a common phenomenon. All you have to do is get a phony style and you can write any amount of words."

Raymond Carver's "minimalism" (I use quotes here because I don't think Carver ever thought of himself as a minimalist) exemplifies this virtue. Look how his story "Vitamins" begins:

> I had a job and Patti didn't. I worked a few hours a night for the hospital. It was a nothing job. I did some work, signed the card for eight hours, went drinking with the nurses. After a while, Patti wanted a job. She said she needed a job for her self-respect. So she started selling multiple vitamins door to door.

Nothing could be simpler than Carver's rhetoric. He says *no* to the typewriter in a way Hemingway would have certainly applauded. But now for a very different approach listen to this:

> On Cader Peak there was a school for witches where the doctor's daughter, teaching the unholy cradle and the devil's pin, had seven country girls. On Cader Peak, half ruined in an enemy weather, the house with a story held the seven girls, the cellar echoing, and a cross reversed above the entrance to the inner rooms. Here the doctor, dreaming of illness, in the centre of the tubercular hill, heard his daughter cry to the power swarming under the West roots. She invoked a particular devil, but the gehenna did not yawn under the hill, and the day and the night continued with their two departures. . . .

This is the beginning of Dylan Thomas' "The School for Witches." Thomas is concerned primarily with the music the language is capable of. The meaning of his story is linked inextricably to the sound of the words. If the sound is wrong, then the meaning is wrong. This is a poet's credo. Thomas is intoxicated by language. He pulls out all the stops and lets fly. The Welsh are great singers, and the music in this passage, as in everything else that Dylan Thomas wrote, is primary.

Dylan Thomas and Ernest Hemingway write from opposite extremes. Both love and respect the language. Thomas gets drunk on it; Hemingway stays sober.

Eudora Welty's prose lies somewhere in between. This is from her story "Death of a Traveling Salesman":

> The cloud floated there to one side like the bolster on his grandmother's bed. It went over a cabin on the edge of a hill, where two bare chinaberry trees clutched at the sky. He drove through a heap of dead oak leaves, his wheels stirring their weightless sides to make a silvery melancholy whistle as the car passed through their bed. No car had been along this way ahead of him. Then he saw that he was on the edge of a ravine that fell away, a red erosion, and that this was indeed the road's end.

There is a *slight* intoxication here, but not of the raving kind. Welty loves words, is not afraid of adjectives or tropes. Hemingway's prose looks for irreducible truth, and distrusts subjective modifiers. Dylan Thomas finds truth in the music of accumulation—words for him are like the notes in a baroque cantata. Eudora Welty finds her accuracy in the selective use of modifiers and metaphors. All three writers are possessed by their own peculiar music.

There are no rights and wrongs here. Hemingway, Thomas, Carver, and Welty are masters. The difference is in style.

STYLE

You've heard a lot about it. Now do this: Forget everything you've heard, including what I'm about to say. Style is not something you want to think about too much. Especially when you are starting out. Style happens. Sometimes it happens early on; sometimes you have to write a few hundred thousand words to find it. (Or for it to find you.) The language you are finally able to use comfortably after much experience, this will be your style. But if you think too hard about it when you're beginning, you're going to write hobbled borrowings that will not have the power to convince.

Here's what Katherine Anne Porter had to say about style: "The style is you. Oh, you can cultivate a style, I suppose, if you like. But I should say it remains a cultivated style. It remains artificial and imposed, and I don't think it deceives anyone. A cultivated style would be like a mask. Everybody knows it's a mask, and sooner or later you must show yourself—or at least you show yourself as someone who could not afford to show himself, and so created something to hide behind. Style is the man." And on the same subject Stendhal, the French novelist who became a major influence on the modern novel, said, "It is the nobility of their style which will make our writers of 1840 unreadable forty years from now." A wonderful caution the budding "stylist" ought to take to heart.

HOW TO READ

When you read other writers, listen closely to the sound their words make—the rhythms and tonalities. Pay attention to how boldly or gingerly they use figures of speech. Acquire a watchdog's alertness for adjectives and adverbs: Do they actually add to the shape and substance of the nouns and verbs they modify, or are they wasted redundancies. Read a page or two out loud. Can you find the rhythm and pace that makes the reading come easy? Do you find yourself possessed by a lovely music, or do you find yourself hacking your way through a hedgerow of tangled syntax?

Read the great masters of this art. Drill their voices into your marrow. And, as you continue to write, read your own work out loud, get a sense of your own music. But don't call it style, don't call it anything. You are, in these moments, paying respects to our language.

Paul Theroux said, "I inhabit every sentence I write." To me, this is the perfect definition of style. It means this: Style is the way a writer sees his or her world. When your sentences are an organic part of your being, then you can call this your "style."

But don't even do that. If your work becomes interesting enough, someone else will take the trouble to do that.

11

REWRITING:
YOUR SECOND, THIRD,
AND TENTH CHANCES

You're taking a midterm test in advanced calculus.

You went to a party the night before and drank too much. You didn't get in until 3 A.M. In fact, you haven't looked at the text in over a week. The weather has been too nice to hole yourself up in your apartment and worry about partial differentials and triple integrals. But you take the test anyway. Your score: 42 percent. A clear and unequivocal F.

But the professor is a nice guy. He wants to help you. He wants you to succeed. He says, "Take another crack at this test next week. Same test, same problems. Study the text a little. See what you can do then."

You thank him. You promise to burn the midnight oil this time. But it's tough sledding. You haven't been the best student. Still, you feel as though you can pass the test, especially now that you know what the problems are in advance.

You take it again. Your score this time is 67. Good enough for a C.

"Do you really want to settle for a C?" the kindly professor asks.

You shrug. No, you'd like a B or an A, but how is that possible? You've had your second chance. Not many professors are so softhearted.

"Look," the professor says. "Take another week to prepare yourself. Then try it again. Same test, same problems. I'd really like to see you do well."

You score an 80 on the third try. The problems are becoming familiar now.

You score an 87 on the fourth try.

By now you are coming up with solutions in your dreams. You recite them at breakfast, at lunch, at dinner. Nobody wants to eat with you anymore. You take the test again. This time you get a 99. An A.

You settle for this. You know that a 100 is too much to hope for, even though the professor is willing to give you another ten chances. A hundred, if you're up for it.

This is exactly what rewriting is all about—second, third and tenth chances to get it right. I use this parable in my beginning classes. Most get the idea, but there are a few holdouts, a few who think that their best work comes immediately and that "tampering" with it only violates the purity of the original inspiration.

These geniuses are the hopeless ones.

In a first draft, I'm never quite sure what I've committed to paper. The characters may be there, the scenes may look good, it all seems to be moving toward some sort of inevitable conclusion, but when I compose that last sentence, I am unconvinced. I long sometimes for the good old days when ". . . and they lived happily ever after" and its modern variations was all a writer needed. The trouble is, stories with tidy endings usually have tidy plots and tidy characters. Too tidy. The stories I want to write deal with contemporary men and women. What could be messier? What subject could have less certainty in its outcome?

One of the fifty-year-old magazines I mentioned in chapter one has a romantic story in it that ends like this.

> She took the step that brought her into his arms. She was laughing and she was crying. "It is, Philip! Oh, it is!" she said.

Never mind what "it" was. They lived happily ever after. They always did. Tidy, very tidy. You can almost see the curtains closing, hear the swelling strains of the string section, the happy tears welling up in the eyes of the satisfied audience.

The readers of magazine fiction fifty years ago wanted tidy endings. They wanted wholesome, life-affirming entertainment. They didn't want to be confused, or disturbed, or left hanging. But contemporary short story writers disturb and confuse and leave you up in the air. They drop the reader into those infinite spaces of Pascal where fear and uncertainty are common denominators. In this world, only zealots have certitude.

Without the help of standard plot devices that make stories easy to conceive, carry out, and conclude, writers often find themselves at sea during composition. And that's as it should be. The world of tidy endings is long gone. The contemporary short story writer, wanting above all to represent life honestly, has to find meanings that are not the ones that were taken for granted in the commercial fiction of fifty years ago. The work has to resonate with the world as we know it. What does this have to do with rewriting? Everything.

The story forms itself, but in that first draft (unless you are very lucky), you won't understand its implications. Before you can let a story go, you have to be able to answer the question, What is my story about? When you can give the answer with some certainty, you can go back and look at each sentence to make sure it contributes to "what the story is about." As Flannery O'Connor said, "The only way, I think, to write short stories is to write them, and then try to discover what you have done."

This is a messy process. It's good to be messy. You have to let fly in that first draft. Words, stacks of them, lovely words, mistaken words, confusing words: Let them roll off your fingertips. The story is forming itself out of chaos. It seems to have direction. It seems to know what it's doing. It has energy, speed, moments of sheer brilliance. But when you've got ten or twenty pages, you've got to stop for breath. You've got to pull yourself out of the dream. It's time to ask the question, *What am I doing?*

It's okay to consider these first pages as a draft. It's probably too early, anyway, to try to make a workable ending. Read those pages, sleep with them, start figuring them out. The solutions will come.

I hope I'm not being too idiosyncratic or obscure about this. I guess I'm telling you my little secrets—how I do it when I'm doing it.

The unconscious mind is your ally. When I was a mathematics major in college, problems I couldn't understand one day sometimes became clear the next. I had to sleep on them; I had to let my brain work in the dark, unharassed by my continuously distracted daylight self.

Maybe you'll come up with a different method. Please understand that what's right for me may not be right for you.

THE HISTORY OF A STORY

I wanted to write a story but I didn't have a subject. (That will happen a lot if you work every day.) So I started writing sentences. I didn't know what I wanted. Out of my emptiness, I began to write about a party my wife and I had at our house. Everyone who came was poor. It was winter. We all wanted to get drunk and have a good time and forget our poverty. Not much grist there for a story.

But I kept writing because that's what I do. The characters began to change from real people to imagined people based on real people. The "I" character, not *me* to begin with, shifted farther away from me-ness. He became an English-as-a-second-language teacher in a community college. My Croatian wife became his Mexican girlfriend. Some people who had never set foot in our house showed up: an amateur magician who was also a job service counselor; a science fiction writer who'd been in jail on a drug charge in L.A.; a one-hundred-year-old man who had witnessed the hanging of a horse thief in the narrator's house before it was a house, when it was a barn; and so on. It grew, the enormous lie grew. It began to make sense to me in some compelling way. They appealed to me, this odd collection of partygoers. There was no plot. No motivating force that I could detect. A religious motif came in from nowhere. It exerted itself. What was going on? Was I losing my grip? But I didn't fight it. (You don't want to fight these visitations, even if they undermine what you believe about yourself. They're telling you something. They keep you honest.)

Oh what a mess I'd made. A story without purpose, a collection of scenes drifting toward some unidentified goal. A horrible spot to put yourself in. But I stayed with it. I liked something about it—the characters, the smoky old house, the good fellowship, the ambient anxiety. I put it away for a while, came back to it, put it away, thought about it. The ending gave me fits. What was the story about? I wrote sentence after sentence, hoping for resonance and meaning, hoping for closure.

I gradually began to see what the story was driving at. While I was doing something else—mowing the lawn, shoveling snow, changing a tire, I don't remember the circumstances now—a line came to me:

> the fragile spray of bones that reached down from her instep and ended at her toes

The line started my mind racing. Then another thought occurred to me: Bones, living bones, are fossils of starlight. That's what we all are, right? Fossils of starlight? From the trillion degree heat of the big bang to the manifold variety of things and creatures of the world, all of it is congealed energy—shapes cut from raw starlight.

What the story was about and the implications of its scenes now hit me like a slap: The party was a gathering of barefoot souls in search of something unknown and unfindable. Here it is.

FEET

Everyone arrived in boots but it was too hot in the house to keep them on. Before long the air was skunky with the intimate aroma of winter feet, feet that had been sealed in leather and thick wool socks all day long.

Most of our guests were half-drunk and in an uncritical frame of mind when they arrived. Those who weren't wearing boots shed their shoes in the spirit of fellowship.

My girlfriend, Rocio Cantú, hated giving parties in this *el norte* country. She claimed she didn't know what white people liked to eat and drink. Even so, this party was her idea. "We *go* to parties, but we never *give* parties," she said, explaining why this one was necessary.

This was a sore point between us. Her reluctance to entertain embarrassed me. We were poor. I'd been out of work for almost a year, having quit my job teaching English as a second language in El Paso.

Rocio was born on a farm in Coahuila but grew up just outside Mexico City. When her family moved to Juárez, she came north. She took my class at the community college, and I fell in love with her. I talked her into moving north with me. "It's better up north," I said. "No hassles, plenty of work, good pay." It was a lie, but I'd been in El Paso for five years and needed a change of scenery. I thought the north Rockies would be good for us.

Throwing parties was an expense our budget couldn't tolerate. I knew this; Rocio knew this. Another thing: whenever we talked about entertaining our friends as potential guests in our house, Rocio suddenly perceived them differently. They were no longer just our friends, but finicky strangers—*guests*. What do you give to a *guest*? Guests are mysteries, they are full of unknown expectations. They come to you wanting happiness and cheer and good times, and how do you provide that?

We are not reasonable people. A few jugs of cheap wine, a pot of something hot—chili, fajitas, gumbo, stew. This takes no monumental effort. Even so, Rocio went catatonic. Such pockets of madness in the woman you live with are not negotiable. They are permanent topographical features of the psyche. You either learn to live with them or they'll rip the bottom out of your love boat. Other things— the good things—even things out. My own unnegotiable psychic topography no doubt gave *her* some troubling thoughts.

Most of our friends were also unemployed. Even so, they are reckless with their food stamps and brought over generous trays of hors d'oeuvres. They even brought booze, an eclectic show of partially filled bottles—vermouth, single grain whiskey, gin, blended rotgut sold only in one-quart bottles, and tequila.

A friend of mine who had just gotten married gave me his old stereo that afternoon, the very afternoon my temperamental old Emerson decided to stop working. His new wife had a brand new Marantz and so he gave me his old Sanyo. It had only one working speaker but that was fine by me. Benny Goodman, Coleman Hawkins, Zoot Sims, Johnny Hodges, Lester Young, Duke Ellington don't require stereo, they come straight at you.

"Good crowd," said Duane Mercator, my counselor from the Unemployment Office. "I see some of them from time to time down at the Job Service. My kind of people."

"Gold bricks to a man," I said, offering him a tray of pumpernickel squares layered with brie and prosciutto.

Duane looked a bit out of place in his blue suit, Paisley tie, and milky, blue-veined feet. Even so he maintained a kind of gloomy dignity that tended to make people keep their distance. He had a lean, hawkish face, the face of a brooding Sicilian, I always thought. Sometimes he seemed more like a Catholic prelate, a man of importance in Holy See politics. Actually, he's an impressively accomplished amateur magician.

"Got any good leads, Duane?" I said.

"Everybody's a teacher in this town, Tony," he said. "This town is swamped with out-of-work professors. The Ph.D. mills are turning them out like Big Macs. McDoctorates are cluttering up the landscape. These people think they're lucky to get hired as adjunct faculty at minimum pay with zilch benefits. And the system is happy to use them. In fact, it feeds on them. These people are vampire meat, Tony."

His eyelids fluttered like willow leaves in a wind when he talked shop. Under the dancing eyelids, his pale gray eyes would travel upward and crescents of the moony, blue-tinged whites would show themselves.

The heavy wet wind of a late winter storm groaned against our little house. Taj Mahal rasped his blues through the single speaker. Morton Arthur, a big man with a ZZ Top beard, gave me a conspiratorial hug. "In your study, man," he said, laying a finger against one side of his ruined nose. I knew what he meant. Morton was connected, and liked to share his coke. He had money to burn, unlike our other guests. He was our local celebrity. Any day now one of his science fiction novels was going to hit the charts. He wrote a kind of juiced-up 1930s space opera with Cyberpunk features: nubile earth women doing crack on the crater-pocked *Pusher Plane-toids*; slave traders providing American teenagers to work the bug farms of the spider people from *The Planet of the Arachnids*; hermaphroditic cowboys herding de-sexed human clones though the underground *Labyrinths of Venus*.

"Feel free," I told him, but in truth I was uncomfortable with his habit. I glanced around the room to see if Rocio was watching. She did not approve of drugs. She always wore the red "I Am Drug Free" ribbon during drug aware-ness week in El Paso.

Mort had been busted in L.A. while working on a screen-play for a mid-budget but never-distributed SF shoot-em-up called *Time Slot*. He'd spent a month in jail, and then six more months doing public service. His public service consisted of lecturing to local high school audiences about the dangers of drugs. Mort loved his drugs, and asking him to denounce them was like asking Jerry Falwell to promote child pornography.

> "Champagne don't make me crazy,
> Cocaine don't make me lazy,
> Ain't nobody's business but my own,"

Morton sang along with Taj Mahal.

Rocio came over to us, suspicious. "No drogs," she said.

"*Deportes sí, drogas no*," Morton said, laughing. It was a bumper sticker we'd brought up from the border. It was on our refrigerator. It tickled Morton. Sports yes, drugs no. "What sports do you play, Rocio?" he said.

In truth, he liked Rocio and Rocio liked him. Their play at hostility was a kind of running joke. But Rocio drew the line at hard drugs. "I mean it, Morton," she said. *No pinchi drogas* in this house."

"Rocio, Rocio, Rocio," Morton intoned, giving her name its rightful Spanish inflections. He passed his middle finger under his nose and inhaled noisily. "I have given up the filthy habit, Rocio. I sniff only *taco pescado* now. It's cheaper and gets you almost as high."

Rocio's eyes got big for a second, then she laughed. "I don't believe you, Morton," she said, cuffing him lightly on the jaw. "You have a filthy mind."

This little house we rent used to be a barn. Legend has it that a horse thief was hanged from its rafters. It's a legend that happens to be true. I call it a legend only because hanged horse thieves in this part of the country are legendary. I found out this piece of history from Peter Selvig, a one-hundred-year-old ex-railroad conductor who lives across the street. He said that he witnessed the hanging. He no longer remembers the name of the thief. He remembers only that the man was tall and skinny and that there was a lot of drunken joking among the grown-ups about whether or not he'd slip the noose when they dropped him. Someone suggested tying a sack of feed to his feet so there'd be enough weight to cinch the noose and snap his neck properly. Peter wasn't supposed to be present—it was strictly a party for adults. But he and his older brother climbed unnoticed up a ladder in the far end of the barn and hid behind a stack of hay in the loft. It was New Year's Eve, 1899, and the thief was to be hanged at the stroke of midnight, ushering in the bright new thief-free century. Peter remembers the condemned man's face clearly as the sheriff's deputy put the noose around his long, thin neck. The expression in the thief's eyes, Peter said, was something to behold. It was calm and peaceful and, in a strange way, *generous*. It suggested something extra-human to little Peter, though he could not have articulated this at the time. The look on the man's face was something Peter could not get out of his mind. It remains vivid almost a century later. Peter, who is on the edge of his own precipice, has something of this same unafraid look. His foggy old eyes are peaceful and generous. "That boy's boots came off," he said. "They tied the mealsack to his boots, and when they dropped him, the sudden stop yanked off his boots. He had little feet, like a girl's." I like Peter a lot and we spend many afternoons in his backyard whittling on pieces of maple. These afternoons are so enjoyable that I'm almost glad to be out of work. *Deportes sí, trabajo no.*

After about six hours the party broke up into sub-parties. There was a group in the bedroom making militia jokes, a north rockies pastime. Three wives sat on the sectional discussing the merits of bulk buying from discount warehouses. Mort Arthur had collected half a dozen people and had taken them into the double-size closet I call my study. I went with these. There were about six of us. "I lied to Rocio," Mort said to me.

He dismantled a picture frame to get at the glass. Then he chopped some generous lines. Someone provided fat Dairy Queen straws that had been clipped short, and we passed the glass around the small room like a communion palette. I was worried Rocio would come in. She had started going to church again after a ten-year layoff and had hung her grandma's old crucifix above our bed—a dark, twisted savior carved out of stubborn mesquite by an eccentric but faithful artisan. Under the black eyes of that Indian Jesus, Rocio was becoming less and less willing to participate in the mild exercises of foreplay. There was no telling what new extreme she might be pushed to if she barged in on Mort's cocaine ceremony.

I went back to the living room, Rocio had gotten uncharacteristically tipsy. Someone had brought a bottle of Irish Cream, and she indulged herself. She likes candy, and Irish Cream is the candy of hard drink. Manitas de Platas, the gypsy guitarist, was on the Sanyo and Rocio, a *mestiza* who claimed three-eighths Spanish blood, was demonstrating the flamenco. For castanets she was using spoons. Her skirts were flying, exposing her long silky thighs and smoky undies. A thin line of sweat gleamed on her temple. Perfume and pheromones mixed and radiated like woodstove heat from her spinning body. *Who is this woman I've tied my life to?* I asked myself, knowing the question was stupid as well as central.

I went into the kitchen where Duane Mercator was doing a magic trick at the insistence of a small crowd. "Everybody sit down and close your eyes," Duane said.

I sat on the floor, back against the wall. A woman I didn't know sat next to me. She offered me a hit from her joint which I refused. "I can't mix my chemicals," I said. She shrugged and passed it the other way. "I'm going to count slowly to ten," Duane said, his voice beautifully modulated. We could have been in Las Vegas, watching an expensive act. His voice was the voice of a professional master of ceremonies. It made you feel that you were in competent hands. You left his cubicle in the Employment Office feeling that important jobs were being lined up for you.

When he finished counting the woman sitting next to me slumped down. The *mota* dropped from her fingers. I picked it up and passed it to my left. I let my head thunk against the wainscoting of the wall behind me, giving in to a sudden post-cocaine fatigue.

Duane said, "I want you to think of a white wall. It's

fifty feet high and a hundred feet wide and it is pure, un-blemished white."

The woman next to me slowly raised her head off the linoleum. "I see it," she said.

"Think of this wall," Duane said, "as a place of complete peace. It is untouched by petty aggravations. No graffiti can mar it. Nothing has ever marred it. It was clean at the beginning of time, it is clean now, and it will be clean at the end of time. It is the wall that surrounds Eden."

"Whoa," said the woman. "I'm going snow blind."

I didn't see any wall. Maybe a pale spot, wide as a quarter. But I had to push it to believe it.

"Try not to be so cynical," Duane said to me. I guess he read the expression on my face.

I made an honest effort. The little pale spot widened. This interested me.

"Now," said Mercator. "Open your eyes."

I opened my eyes. The pale spot was still there. Not fifty feet tall, but definitely there. Mercator opened the oven door. He took a bottle of milk out of the fridge and put it into the oven. He turned the oven on and set the dial to "Bake."

"I'm going to start counting again," he said. "When I reach twenty, I'll open the oven. He reached twenty, then opened the door again. The bottle of milk was gone. In its place was a package. Duane took the package out and removed the heavy brown wrapping paper that covered it. He tore the paper off the package and opened the box. A kitten raised its head and mewed. Duane closed the oven door. He counted to twenty again. Then he opened the oven again. Inside was the bottle of milk. He got a saucer out of the cupboard and poured some milk into it. I could see, from the way it steamed, that it was warm milk. The kitten ran to the saucer and began lapping it up, her tail erect and quivering with pleasure. We applauded.

I got up and went back into the front room. For some

reason, Duane's magic trick had bothered me. The white haze he'd called up was still with me. It flared around the living room like a halo. Rocio had finished dancing and was now sitting on the sofa sipping Irish Cream.

I went down to the basement to lie down and watch television, hoping the party would break up pretty soon. I watched part of a T and A movie on the Playboy channel. Then I switched to one of the Christian channels where a pair of evangelists, a man and a woman, told their audience how at one time they did not have a measurable ounce of faith. "Hey!" the woman cried out with the élan of a cheerleader, "Look how far we *come!*"

I slept for a while. When I woke, the party was over, our guests were gone. I found Rocio sitting on the floor of the shower stall. She sat with her knees pulled up, her arms crossed on her knees, her head on her arms, while tepid water lashed her brown back, the knuckles of her spine shining like wet stones.

I turned off the water. "Come on, let's go to bed, honey," I said.

She sobbed. One big, ragged sob. This is where she goes when she is sad, the shower. I lifted her up and held her against my chest. Her breasts turn outward in their fullness. I read that somewhere once—a generously erotic phrase— and it applies to Rocio. When she got her feet under her, I wrapped her in a towel.

I locked up the house and we went to the bedroom. She collapsed on the bed in a careless sprawl—her thighs loose in a parody of invitation. I knew from experience that it would have been a mistake to misread the moment. I left her there, her eyes half open, her mind halfway back to the slopes of Chapultepec.

I cleaned up the house, put the coke-dusty glass back into the picture frame, washed the dishes. When I went back to the bedroom, Rocio was kneeling at the head of the bed, kissing the gnarled mesquite feet of her grandmother's

Jesus. She was still weeping, silently, and I knew that we would soon be going back to the border.

I knelt beside the bed, stroked her calves and her feet. They were perfect feet—long, narrow, highly arched. I traced the delicate webbing of veins under the transparent skin, the bleak and startling rise of the ankles.

As she kissed the feet of her grandmother's Jesus, I kissed the fragile spray of bones that reached down from her instep and ended at her toes: for they too were fossils of starlight that had not forgotten their radiant freedom.

The mystical and humble beauty of feet and the unfulfilled spiritual needs of ordinarily skeptical people—that's what I came to believe the story was about.

The false thrill of magic—false, yet the guests flock to the magician, looking for something to believe in. And the fleeting ecstasy of drugs, how they mimic spiritual experience—it was about these things, too.

And this: Rocio's lovely feet and the hard scrabble feet of the mesquite Christ became humble emblems of our common humanity: rich or poor, we haven't got much.

What an odd thing to be writing about. I can't account for the odd things I write, but I don't apologize for them, either. Nor should you. Stories happen. They happen, gradually, in the rewrites.

"Feet" has no plot worthy of the name, no serious crisis, very little in the way of conflict, not much of a resolution—just an evening of aimless partying. Yet it is a story; it even has an epiphany. The epiphany came to me while I was mowing the lawn, shoveling snow, or changing a tire.

As I wrote the story through the several drafts, my sense of what it was about grew stronger. I began to shape some of the images and scenes to fit what I saw as the story's "plan." The cocaine scene became an act of communion. Duane Mercator, the employment counselor, seems, to the narrator, like a Catholic prelate, a man of importance in Holy See politics. The hypnotic trance he induces creates the white walls of Eden in the minds of his audience, perhaps taking them back to original innocence. Peter, the old man, seems acquainted and at home with death, his eyes peaceful and generous. Then the narrator, channel surfing, momentarily tunes in a pair of shouting evangelists. Finally, the image of homesick Rocio, kissing the feet of Jesus, and the narrator kissing Rocio's feet, the "fossils of starlight." The erotic and the spiritual momentarily connected. It all fit together as a piece. In my mind, anyway.

When I started the story, I had no conscious intention of dealing with such a subject. But when I understood where the story was heading, I accepted it. What else can you do?

What you set out to do is not all that important. What is important is what develops along the way. The way is hard, and may require many rewrites, but if there is something there in the first place, it will emerge.

THE RISKS OF HONEST WRITING

One of the risks of fiction writing is the discoveries you might make. Set a character on some small odyssey and he or she may surprise you in ways you did not want to be surprised. My poetry writing teacher emphasized this above all. Suppose, he said, you set out to write a poem against war. It's going along well, the images are stacking up nicely, your point is being made with conviction and force. Then disaster strikes: A line comes to you, a line that seems inevitable, given what has come before it. This line implicates you in a way you did not want to be implicated. Say the line goes something like this:

I grieve for them with stones in my hands.

You like this line a lot. It resonates with the line before it, but it suggests a direction the poem might take, a direction that worries you. The line is warlike in character, disturbingly aggressive, but you like it anyway. It *sounds* right—there's a nice internal rhyme connecting it to the previous line:

In their graves those young bones grow wise.

You don't want to lose that "bones-stones" rhyme. But damn—the poem is implicating the poet! It exposes you as "red in tooth and claw," just another killer among killers. What are you going to do about this? How can you maintain your moral invulnerability when the thing you're writing is pointing the finger at *you*?

The choice is simple: Go with it, accept the implications of that line, or *don't write it*—write instead something that agrees with your initial high-minded intention.

> I grieve for them, my hands empty and clean.

This takes you off the hook; it certifies your virtue. But it's a lie. It violates the direction your intuition told you the poem wanted to take. The line that was inevitable has been replaced by a line that is merely acceptable—but it's a damn *lie*.

A fiction writer faces the same kind of moral choice. Sometimes your intuition will turn a story in a direction that disturbs you. You expected to do one thing, but now you're doing another. You had a plan, an intention, but it's been violated. You're now heading into uncharted waters.

Chekhov, criticizing a writer who wrote from a narrow agenda, said, "He finds truth under the rock where he had previously hidden it." When you know what you're going to find, you're playing it safe.

The truth is always surprising. When you stumble across it, don't flinch. When it unearths itself before you, seize it. It's what you've been looking for.

GRAINS OF SALT

Reading back over these pages, I realize that what I've been saying is idiosyncratic in many ways. It reflects what I've come to understand about writing short stories over the last few decades. And I repeat now what I said in chapter one: *I don't know how to write short stories.* (I've written hundreds, I expect to write hundreds more—but that doesn't count. When I'm *between* stories, the old fears and doubts come back: How do I *do* this? How does *anyone* do this?) Though I know more now than I did thirty years ago, I'm still as mystified by the process as I was when I started out. There is no "way" to write short stories. If there were, the art would be dead and gone. It's good to be mystified. It means you hold the subject in awe.

It's possible that what I've learned is not what you have learned, or what you will come to learn in the future. That's fine. In fact, that's how it should be. We share a language but within that single commonality each of us must find his or her own methods.

You should know this, too: Short stories don't get easier to write as you mature as a writer. In fact, they get harder. I speak only for myself, but I've yet to meet a writer who claims writing gets easier with years.

I just had dinner with an old friend, a writer, who confided in me that he can't write the story until he has realized it fully beforehand in his mind. This is exactly what I advised you against, and yet my friend is a fine short story writer. Another friend of mine hangs a chart on his wall and "maps out" his novels before daring to begin. I write novels in the way I write short stories—following my headlights in the dark, knowing I can drive across the country that way. If I wrote a book on how to write the novel, I'd advise against planning it out. To some aspiring novelists, this would be bad advice.

And yet another friend of mine claims he takes "dictation." He actually *hears* the story in his head, and he writes it down as hard and as fast as he can. It's as if the story is being delivered to him. I was having lunch with him once and suddenly he stopped eating and talking. He froze. We'd been having a good time but now he looked distressed, as if he were having stomach cramps. "I've got to go, man," he said. "Where?" I said. "You haven't finished your burrito." He didn't answer. He didn't need to. I knew what was happening to him. His muse was whispering sweet somethings in his ear.

My friend amazes me; he makes me envious, too. My muse doesn't whisper to me. She pulls me out of bed now and then at 3 A.M. and makes me jot down scraps of dialogue, description, and story ideas, but that's about it. I'm jealous of my friend's tight relationship with his muse. How come he gets special treatment?

Of all I've said, I know only one thing that is infallibly true for all of us: In order to write, you must write. You must sit down and put words on paper on a somewhat regular basis whether you hear them in your head or pull them one by one from your brain by their bloody roots.

I assume you have the other necessities—the love of language, the love of stories, the need to write.

Some students I've encountered aren't sure about their need. There's a simple test for that. Answer the question, Can you live without it? Can you turn your back on it and take up some other, less punishing pursuit? If the answer is yes, then this is exactly what you should do. If you *can* quit, you should. I give this advice to all my students, from rank beginners to graduate M.F.A. students. I think it's good advice, even valuable advice. I think it saves them a lot of unnecessary grief.

This book is addressed and dedicated to all of you who *can't* quit, who would be miserable if denied pencil, pen, or keyboard.

Oh yes, it's a *calling*, no doubt about it.

ABOUT THE AUTHOR

Rick DeMarinis has taught fiction writing at the University of Montana, San Diego State University, Arizona State University, and at the University of Texas at El Paso. He has received a literary award from the American Academy and Institute of Arts and Letters as well as two National Endowment for the Arts fellowships. He has published six novels and five collections of stories. His stories have been published in *Harper's*, *The Atlantic*, *Esquire*, *GQ*, *Story*, *The Paris Review*, and others. He retreated from teaching in 1999 in order to write full-time.

INDEX